What is
Cultural Sociology?

What is Sociology? Series

What is Cultural Sociology?

LYN SPILLMAN

polity

First published in 2020 by Polity Press

Polity Press
65 Bridge Street
Cambridge CB2 1UR, UK

Polity Press
101 Station Landing
Suite 300
Medford, MA 02155, USA

ISBN-13: 978-1-5095-2280-4
ISBN-13: 978-1-5095-2281-1 (pb)

A catalogue record for this book is available from the British Library.

Library of Congress Cataloging-in-Publication Data
Names: Spillman, Lyn, author.
Title: What is cultural sociology? / Lyn Spillman.
Description: Cambridge, UK ; Medford, MA : Polity, 2020. | Series: What is sociology? series | Includes bibliographical references and index. | Summary: "Offering a concise answer to the question "What is Cultural Sociology?," this book provides an overview of what you need to know to do cultural sociology. Spillman demonstrates many of the conceptual tools cultural sociologists use to help understand how people make meaning, with vivid examples from this rich and ubiquitous feature of our lives"-- Provided by publisher.
Identifiers: LCCN 2019024009 (print) | LCCN 2019024010 (ebook) | ISBN 9781509522804 (hardback) | ISBN 9781509522811 (paperback) | ISBN 9781509522842 (epub)
Subjects: LCSH: Culture.
Classification: LCC HM621 .S653 2020 (print) | LCC HM621 (ebook) | DDC 301--dc23
LC record available at https://lccn.loc.gov/2019024009
LC ebook record available at https://lccn.loc.gov/2019024010

Typeset in 10.5 on 12pt Sabon
by Fakenham Prepress Solutions, Fakenham, Norfolk NR21 8NL
Printed and bound in the UK by TJ International Limited

For further information on Polity, visit our website: politybooks.com

Contents

Acknowledgments

I am grateful for all my many encounters and conversations over the years with cultural sociologists who have developed the field from its inception to its diversity and strength today. They have made cultural sociology an intellectual home I could not have imagined when I first wondered long ago why sociologists did not seem to talk about culture. Among all these colleagues over the years, I have been particularly fortunate in the support, encouragement, and friendship of Jeffrey Alexander, Nina Eliasoph, Paul Lichterman, and Ann Swidler, even though each of them might well critique the picture of the field presented in this book.

I also thank Jonathan Skerrett, who motivated the project, Karina Jákupsdóttir, for her patience in seeing it through, and Justin Dyer, for his impressive copy-editing. The manuscript benefited from the comments of three anonymous reviewers. Michael Strand also offered helpful comments. Colleagues and students in Sociology at the University of Notre Dame create a stimulating environment for doing cultural sociology, and certainly enriched the picture presented here in many ways. Rebecca Overmyer provided enormous help by preserving time for this work among other responsibilities. Rachel Keynton, Robert Mowry, and Lilly Watermoon contributed essential background research at different stages of the project. I benefited from extended critical conversation on many of the topics included here with participants in my cultural sociology seminars. Especially fond thanks go to the seventy students who have worked with me over the years in preparation for advanced field examinations: I always finish our meetings feeling privileged by the opportunity. Russell Faeges helps in all these ways and many more and I thank him, too, for his sustained support.

1
Introduction

Sociology teaches us about human groups and human interactions, how they work, and how they influence our lives.
Cultural sociology investigates the meanings people attach
to their groups and interactions. What do their groups mean
to people, where do those various meanings come from, and
how do those meanings influence what they do?

For all of us as human creatures, meaning is as essential
to our existence as infant care or water. Our lives are full
of meaning and meaning-making. Sometimes our ideas and
values are totally taken for granted. We are supported and
sustained by perceptions of the world which seem natural
and inevitable, passed on to us implicitly by those who raise
us. Our meaning-making is like breathing, and we don't
notice the air that surrounds us.

At other times – and more and more often – we encounter
different ideas about what is really meaningful. Encountering
differences can be fascinating and helps us learn more about
ourselves. Sometimes, though, cultural differences may give
us "culture shock," and disagreements challenging the ideas
we take for granted may seem like "culture wars." Modern
life makes escalating cultural difference unavoidable, even
as it also offers exponentially increasing opportunities for
sharing meaning through mass and social media.

Cultural sociology offers concepts and methods to help
explore meaning-making – familiar meanings we share,

strange and unfamiliar meanings, and those we dispute with others. To start noticing the meaning-making all around us, we can orient ourselves by thinking about different rituals, symbols, values, norms, and categories.

Rituals, symbols, values, norms, and categories

As big, splashy, intentional, repetitive events distinct from everyday life, *rituals* clearly highlight culture and cultural difference. Weddings, graduations, pep rallies, religious services, birthday celebrations, and patriotic holidays – all of these are ritual events expressing the meanings of our social relationships. For example, new family commitments are expressed in wedding rituals, and shared national identity is expressed in patriotic holidays like July 4th or Bastille Day.

Because rituals are intentionally distinct from everyday life, they make cultural differences obvious. For instance, while graduations everywhere mark students' transitions to the social status of graduate, different peoples do graduations differently. In New Zealand, unlike elsewhere, a university graduation begins with a traditional Maori welcome, with a Maori man blowing a conch shell, and a "Kairanga," or call, by two Maori women in traditional dress. The chancellor of the university then offers a welcome in the Maori language, before the graduation ceremony proceeds much as it would anywhere else in the English-speaking world. To take another example of the ways ritual highlights cultural difference, even though national holidays everywhere celebrate history and patriotism, Norway's "Children's Parade," coordinated by schools in every town (Elgenius 2011, 119–22), looks different to July 4th fireworks in the United States, or the glamorous military parades and local fire-station dances of France's Bastille Day. Other peoples' rituals condense cultural difference and draw attention to stories and symbols their participants may take for granted as "natural." They may also condense unfamiliar histories and traces of conflict – highlighting, for instance, the residual effects of Maori resistance to the white ("pakeha") invasion of New Zealand in the mid-nineteenth century, or, in Norway, strategic efforts to claim Norwegian identity and independence from Sweden later in that century (Elgenius 2011, 119).

Sometimes, too, conflict and disagreement over meaning become vivid in ritual processes. A protest march with large signs and chants dramatizes political dispute. So too do celebrities wearing colors or badges supporting controversial causes while they announce prizewinners at the Oscars.

Whatever the mix of consensus, difference, and dispute in big ritual events, they make vivid assertions about the meanings of our groups and social relationships and demonstrate cultural difference. But cultural differences extend beyond the bright highlights of unfamiliar ritual. Moving into any new setting, we also encounter less obvious differences to surprise us.

We encounter different *symbols*. Language is often an obvious symbolic difference, but even if we share a language, new vocabulary and diction can make communicating with someone from a different subculture or region a little strange. (Should you be asking for a "soda," "pop," "cool drink," "soft drink," or even "frappé"? What exactly is a "freshman"?) And symbolic differences run much deeper than language. Many symbols are highlighted in ritual events – such as team mascots, religious images, and national flags. But symbolism also pervades everyday life. Uniforms symbolize membership of teams, schools, the military, and many workplaces. T-shirts emblazon us with our tastes and tribes. Different genders are symbolized by different clothes almost everywhere. (Why don't most men wear skirts in Western countries? What's the point of high heels?) Even simple colors can mean different things. (Is black more associated with death than white, or vice versa? What are the different meanings of wearing a pink ribbon, a red ribbon, or a yellow ribbon?) And consumerism creates an even more complex symbolic universe. (Which sneakers will convey the best impression?)

Shared symbols ease communication, but we hesitate and puzzle over symbols that are new to us. We might ask for an explanation of a military medal, or an unfamiliar image on a road sign or a coin or a t-shirt. If we encounter symbols that are too unfamiliar – like the social difference between wearing a toga and a tunic in ancient Rome, or the lined and dotted rock paintings of Aboriginal groups – we need to learn the meanings just as we might learn a new language. And beyond taken-for-granted consensus and unfamiliar cultural difference, symbols express power, challenge, and conflict. Crowns and private airplanes are symbols of power. A rainbow flag makes a symbolic challenge to public assumptions about sexuality. Large neighborhood murals in Belfast or Chicago are permanent reminders of longstanding political tensions.

Noticing rituals and symbols like these – our own, and those of other people – helps us reflect on culture and helps to orient us to cultural sociology. Some other common ideas are equally helpful: we can also orient ourselves to culture by thinking about values, norms, and categories.

When we evaluate something as good or bad, something else as better or worse, we are making meaning about values, and these *evaluations* are often moral judgements. People appeal to "family values," or the value of "education," and they may value "tradition" or "innovation." What exactly these values mean in practice is often vague, and how values are applied can shift with social context. For example, do we expect "family values" to include an extended family of second cousins and great aunts, or are they restricted to the straight nuclear family? Is it controversial to include gay couples and their children? (For this reason, cultural sociologists have recently preferred to investigate the sociology of evaluation, rather than using the more static concept of values.) Regardless of how values are applied in practice, though, people often draw boundaries between themselves and others, "us" and "them," on the basis of such moral evaluations. And along with moral evaluations, aesthetic evaluations, like taste in music, are also important for making judgements and defining groups. In fact, cultural sociologists have shown that aesthetic values are often closely linked to moral judgements, and equally important in defining group identities.

Subtle cultural differences can often be seen in differing evaluations. Some people judge whether their acquaintances are better or worse than themselves according to the size and quality of their residence. Others make the same judgement on the basis of their tastes in music or movies.

And sometimes value differences and change generate cultural conflicts, as when women executives must try to reconcile conflicts between values of family responsibilities and work commitment. Conversely, male homemakers may be stigmatized by their peers as "unsuccessful" if they choose devotion to home and family over an intense ethic of paid work. More generally, some of the most difficult forms of political conflict are expressed as value differences, like conflicts between egalitarian and authoritarian political values, or conflicts between economic and environmental assessments of new mining projects.

So we can become more attuned to big cultural differences by observing rituals, symbols, and evaluations wherever we are. We can also start to see intriguing cultural differences if we observe social *norms*. What do people take for granted about their interactions? Norms are often taken for granted – we fail to notice them until something goes wrong. If you move from a big city to a small town, it may seem odd that strangers greet you on the street – they seem to be violating interactional norms common in city life about keeping yourself to yourself. In the same way, bargaining over price, displays of affection, or interrupting a conversation are all normative in some settings, but offensive in others. Subtle patterns of interaction may seem trivial, but we learn their importance for meaning-making when they are breached.

Even more subtle are the taken-for-granted *categories* we use to divide up the world. Categories help clarify fuzzy perception, removing confusion and ambiguity. Clear categorization makes perception and action easier. An experienced chess player, familiar with categories of chess pieces like "queen" and "pawn," will more easily remember a game layout than someone who doesn't know a queen from a pawn, to whom all games will look much the same. Company stocks which fall between market categories do not do as well on the market as stocks which can be clearly categorized (Hsu et al. 2009; Zuckerman 2004).

On a larger scale, categories are always important cultural elements because social groups often vary in the ways they categorize the same reality, and their various cultural categories are consequential. For instance, when exactly you become an "adult" can vary widely. Are you an adult at fifteen or twenty-five? Are you an adult when you can fight in a war, bear children, hold a bar mitzvah or *quinceañera*, drive, drink, graduate, vote, earn your living, or form a new family yourself? "Childhood," "adolescence," "adulthood," and "old age" are socially defined categories that make fundamental differences in our lives (Benedict 1959 [1934]; Furstenburg et al. 2004). To take another example, what work is categorized as "professional"? We might take it for granted that medicine and law are usually seen as professions, but what about artists or childcare workers? Whether or not a job is categorized as a profession is socially defined, and the categorization makes a difference for workers and clients (Spillman and Brophy 2018).

Cultural challenges and conflicts frequently target social categories, too. Older people might challenge regulations that make them "too old" to drive, and childcare workers might organize to become a profession. By looking at categories we take for granted, we can attune ourselves to observe another important type of cultural difference.

So to investigate culture, cultural difference, and cultural conflict, we need to stop taking meaning-making for granted. Thinking about elements of culture – like rituals, symbols, values, norms, and categories – provides a vocabulary and an orientation with which to become more mindful of meaning-making in all its vast variation. Having initiated a more mindful attention to cultural elements surrounding us and cultural differences we encounter, we are in a better position to analyze and understand them.

The idea of culture

Many generations of scholars have sought to understand culture, cultural difference, and cultural conflict. Before turning to contemporary cultural sociology, it is helpful to deepen our initial orientation to the idea of culture by considering how it emerged and how it was taken up in sociology. The idea of culture carries historical connotations which echo around contemporary approaches. This historical baggage explains why some people say the idea of culture is confusing. Unpacking the baggage clarifies what we think of when we think of culture and shows how contemporary cultural sociology's conceptual tools help specify and focus cultural explanation.

The contemporary idea of "culture" emerged in Europe as a way of characterizing differences between human groups, and changes within them. We know relatively little about pre-modern and non-Western understandings of what we would now call cultural difference. Among the ideas that survive, and are viewed as prefiguring contemporary cultural investigation, the ancient Greek historian Herodotus (c. 485–c. 425 BCE) is remembered for his careful observation and analysis of differences between different groups and regions in their everyday practices, including food, clothing, gender relations, sexual behavior, religion, and military organization, recognizing that "practices and norms which one nation may regard as right and proper may be considered outlandish and even shocking by another" (Evans 1982, 40; see also Ginzburg 2017). North African scholar and political leader Ibn Khaldun (1332–1406) is admired for his *Muqaddimah*, or "introduction to history," in which he analyzed *asabiyyah* (social cohesion or group solidarity) – which is stronger in nomadic, tribal societies compared to complex societies with central government – thus outlining an original theory of the role of culture in society (Çaksu 2017; Dhaouadi 1990; Gellner 1988). Europeans around Ibn Khaldun's time often followed the classical geographical tradition, in which the physical environment caused social traits which were passed on to future generations – so, for instance, groups from harsh regions developed harsh characters. But one early geographer, Nicolas de Nicolay, after travelling with a French ambassador in the Ottoman Empire in 1551, abandoned this geographical determinism for a more modern attention to socialization, situated action, and social engineering (Mukerji 2013).

Raymond Williams, a twentieth-century British sociologist, literary critic, novelist, and activist, traced the European development of ideas about culture from around this time in the sixteenth century in his investigation of "keywords" (Williams 1976). According to Williams, the idea of culture emerged in the English Renaissance as a noun of process. At first, "culture" referred to the process of nurturing crops or animals, but the reference was gradually extended from agricultural husbandry to human development, as in the "culture" of skills, or the soul. This extension of the idea of active cultivation to human development from husbandry accompanied shifting ideas about responsibility for human nature, from religion and metaphysics to humanity itself. In this early phase, "culture" as a process always implied the cultivation of something, whether crops or skills.

But after the Industrial Revolution, from the late eighteenth century, "culture" began to refer to a general human feature, an institution, or a property of whole groups: an abstract thing more than an active process. By the mid-nineteenth century, in the English language, "culture" contrasted moral and intellectual activities with emerging economic and political trends in capitalism, industry, democracy, and revolution. This marked a stronger practical separation of ideas, ideals, and arts from other important economic and political activities and powers then disrupting traditional society. "Culture" became a court of appeal set against economic and political changes, a basis for value judgements made by English Romantic writers and others critical of the Industrial Revolution. "Culture" as an abstract quality of inner or spiritual development separated the arts, religion, and other institutions and practices of meaning and value from economic and political institutions and practices. British educator Matthew Arnold, for example, argued in 1869 that "culture," considered as sensitivity and flexible judgement informed by the arts and humanities, could be an antidote to the destructive materialism of modernity (Eagleton 2000, 11; Griswold 2013, 4–5). This historical genealogy still influences us when we think of the arts and popular culture as distinct from – perhaps "higher" and "purer" than – economic and political processes.

Meanwhile, increasing European awareness of other peoples and exploration and conquest around the globe created a different, more comparative set of connotations to the idea of culture. The culture concept was used to emphasize and analyze differences among human populations. Especially for German thinkers such as eighteenth-century philosopher Johann Gottfried von Herder, "culture" became associated with the "whole way of life" of a group (Eagleton 2000,

12–13, 26). Sometimes, different cultures were seen as representing different stages of human progress, traceable through such features as means of subsistence, arts, beliefs, and religion (Kroeber and Kluckhohn 1963 [1952], 32). However, from the late nineteenth century, anthropologists pluralized and relativized the idea, recognizing that different cultures could not be evaluated according to a simple hierarchy – "culture" became "cultures" considered of equal value. This plural, relative, comparative sense of culture as a whole way of life was foundational in anthropology (Benedict 1959 [1934]; Kuper 1999; Ortner 1984; Stocking 1968).

This genealogy is still influential for popular understanding of "culture," too. We are now very familiar with the idea that cultures are diverse, and similarly we usually assume that cultural possibilities are innumerable, that elements of a culture form interrelated patterns, and that these elements need to be placed in context to be understood. We might travel to experience "a different culture," or celebrate diverse "cultures" in a city festival. These connotations all developed in anthropology and spread into common usage by the mid-twentieth century.

Because of this complex genealogy, the idea of culture is often used in quite different ways, even by the same person. Sometimes, following the first historical thread, you may use the term to refer to a distinct institutional realm of arts and humanities, different from – and maybe lesser or greater than – "practical" realms of politics and economics. At other times, following the second historical thread, you may use the term to characterize whatever is shared by a whole group, in contrast to other groups. Simply recognizing the genealogy of these connotations can help eliminate unnecessary confusion and ambiguity.

Culture in sociology

Until later in the twentieth century, sociologists also used the idea of culture quite loosely and ambiguously. Because, as Robert Nisbet has argued, "sociology, more than any other discipline, has taken on the conflicts between traditionalism and modernism in European culture" (1993 |1966|, vii), culture was often seen in the first sense, as a separate realm of human life. On the other hand, the popularization of the anthropological idea that culture is a property distinguishing whole groups also influenced sociology, to the extent that twentieth-century sociology textbooks referred to "the anthropological idea of culture" for many years.

But even though sociology (unlike anthropology) was vague on the concept of culture for a long time, similar ideas flourished in other ways. All the classic sociological theorists were writing when the idea of culture was in flux, so they did not offer paradigmatic approaches to understanding "culture." Nevertheless, all of them bequeathed related ideas and theoretical propositions that remain crucial, combining in different ways in later cultural sociology. Karl Marx showed how meaning-making could be important for domination, with his concept of ideology (Marx 1978 [1846]; see also Eagleton 1991; Wuthnow 1992). Max Weber established an important place for interpretive analysis in sociology and offered particular theories of social status and of historical rationalization which remain influential for cultural sociology (Weber 1998 [1904–5]; see also Schroeder 1992). Émile Durkheim provided the foundations of cultural analysis in sociology with his theories of collective conscience, collective representations, cognitive categories, and ritual (Durkheim 1995 [1912]; see also Alexander and Smith 2005). Georg Simmel contributed extensive reflections on the individual's relation to surrounding culture by distinguishing objective and subjective culture (Simmel 1971; see also Frisby and Featherstone 1997). However, while all offered useful ways of thinking about cultural elements like rituals, symbols, evaluations, norms, and categories, they mostly did so only as a sideline in the course of answering other sorts of questions.

In the 1960s, a sociological best-seller encapsulated a fundamental cultural insight in its title – the central idea of "the social construction of reality." Authors Peter Berger and Thomas Luckmann aimed to provide a "sociological analysis of the reality of everyday life" (1966, 19). They applied insights from the twentieth-century sociology of knowledge, formerly devoted to what they called "theoretical thought," to mundane settings – "what people 'know' as 'reality' in their everyday non- or pre-theoretical lives" (1966, 15). For this they drew on the phenomenologist Alfred Schutz for insight on common sense; they followed Weber's emphasis on subjective meanings; they adopted some of Durkheim's ideas about the impact of "social facts" for the individual; they modified Durkheim's view with a more dynamic idea of dialectical influence between individual and society that they attributed to Marx; and they used George Herbert Mead's symbolic interactionist understanding of socialization (Berger and Luckmann 1966, 16–17). Even though they avoided developing the concept of culture, their well-known work provided an undisputed position statement for sociologists interested in culture, cultural difference, and cultural conflict. The platform they offered for understanding meaning-making was widely adopted in sociology, and, as a result, what came to be called "social constructionism" came to be taken as sociological common ground (Vera 2016; for an extended critical assessment see Smith 2010, 119–206).

For Berger and Luckmann, structured patterns of social relations in groups are internalized by individuals in everyday life, and individuals then reproduce and sometimes change those patterns. For instance, an individual might internalize hierarchical family relations and then go on to live them out anew. Internalization is mediated by "signs" generated by surrounding social relations. So a child might understand family hierarchy through practical signs of interactional deference or explicit symbols of authority. This perspective on "the social construction of reality" synthesized disparate strands of social theory, from the macro to the micro – theories of objective social structure, theories of interaction, and phenomeno-logical theories of subjective experience. Essentially, Berger and Luckmann offered a distinctively sociological vocabulary for understanding processes of meaning-making – in other words, for understanding "culture."

So although sociologists were often vague about the concept of culture through the mid-twentieth century, they came to view what were essentially cultural processes through the lens of concepts like "ideology," "collective conscience," "interpretation," and "the social construction of reality." For some sociologists, the widespread acceptance of these ideas resolved uncertainties about analyzing culture. For many others, though, ideas like "the social construction of reality" were useful as signposts but opened more issues than they resolved. How does the dialectical social construction of reality operate in practice? What does this idea suggest about how to do sociological research on culture?

One intransigent issue was a theoretical impasse between conflict and consensus views of culture, between an emphasis on power and conflict, captured in the concept of ideology, and an emphasis on solidarity and consensus, as in the concept of collective conscience. Another recurring tension surrounded whether to focus on the influence of social structures (recurrent patterns of social relations) or on interactional processes (in which human agency and creativity might sometimes be seen). A third issue revolved around whether to highlight the interpretation of meanings themselves (as Weber did, for example, in his famous study of the Protestant Ethic [1998 (1904–5)]) or whether a genuinely sociological approach should minimize extended, thick interpretation of rituals, symbols, evaluations, norms, and categories and focus instead on external social forces which might explain them. These persistent issues – conflict vs. consensus, structure vs. agency, and interpretation vs. explanation – were all the more intransigent for sociologists interested in culture because "culture" was understood in broad, abstract terms as reflecting whole societies. Inquiries into such broad, abstract topics as "American culture" make it hard to even begin to answer specific questions about meaning-making.

From the 1970s, though, and in the process of dealing with these questions, sociologists stopped treating the idea of culture as vague and residual, as an abstract thing, and explicitly specified concepts and approaches to understanding culture, cultural difference, and cultural conflict. The thriving field of cultural sociology emerged.

Cultural sociology and processes of meaning-making

So several sources of confusion can make the idea of culture seem unclear, especially in sociology. Not only is there extreme real-world variation in particular rituals, symbols, evaluations, norms, and categories we may encounter, there are also many options and debates about how to analyze them. Moreover, the historical genealogy of the idea of culture still generates two distinct connotations: culture as a separate institutional sphere within modern societies (highlighting differences with economics and politics); and culture as a property of whole social groups (highlighting social differences). And beyond that, disputes within sociology about whether to emphasize cultural conflict or consensus, social structure or agency, and interpretation or explanation added a further layer of complexity to thinking about culture, including different vocabularies to understand cultural elements. As a result, sociologists have occasionally complained that culture is so complicated and confusing that it is impossible to analyze. But this complaint makes little sense: any topic can be complex and ambiguous when we start to dig deep, even topics that some would consider easier to study, like politics or economics. What is needed is a sociological concept of culture which offers coherence in complexity. Since the seventies, cultural sociologists have been working with just such a concept.

All cultural sociology shares a central focus on *processes of meaning-making*. Cultural sociologists investigate puzzles and questions about meanings, and in doing so they account for the various rituals, symbols, evaluations, norms, and categories that people may share, and take for granted as natural. They also offer a fresh understanding of how taken-for-granted ideas may generate power, inequality, and conflict. Meaning-making processes generate both pattern and variation.

This concept of culture, referring to processes of meaning-making, actually returns to and extends what Raymond Williams found to be the first uses of the concept as a noun of process, before "culture" was reified as a unitary, abstract thing. Since the term is now understood to refer to a process, it can encompass various elements, because meaning may be generated and expressed in ritual, symbolization, evaluation, normative action, and categorization (and numerous other cultural processes).

The concept of culture as meaning-making process also works well to include both historical connotations of the term: meaning-making processes are involved whether our analytic focus is on culture as a distinct set of social institutions producing symbolic objects (arts, popular culture, mass culture, etc.) or on culture as a property of groups (and characterizing group differences).

Within sociology, considering culture as meaning-making process highlights what different approaches and perspectives share, while remaining open to different views about the nature of the processes involved. It bears a close relationship to the Berger and Luckmann idea of "the social construction of reality," which sociologists generally embraced, but makes conceptual space for more analytical precision and flexibility, opening social construction up to analysis, rather than closing it down as a generic sociological assumption about "reality." And it allows us to take a step back from overarching sociological debates about conflict and consensus, structure and agency, and interpretation and explanation, capturing an idea common to them all and turning those debates into specific empirical questions, like "what is the mix of conflict and consensus in this situation, and why?" And as this book will show, the concept of culture as meaning-making process also encompasses more recent perspectives within cultural sociology about how to study culture.

However, all investigations begin with presuppositions, and it is helpful to make them explicit. The major presuppositions of cultural sociology are captured in the foundational concept of meaning. Cultural sociologists assume that humans are meaning-making creatures and that meaning is an essential component of all human groups and human action. Meaning is understood as distinct from biological processes: although meaning-making is certainly an emergent natural capacity of humans as biological creatures, and biology and culture can influence each other, meaning is not reducible to biological processes. Meaning is also understood as fundamentally public: although individual, subjective experience is certainly essential in meaning-making, meaning is not reducible to that experience. Rather, collective meaning-making processes create the conditions for individual, subjective experience. These presuppositions – that humans are meaning-making creatures, that culture is irreducible to biology, and that meaning is irreducible to private, subjective experience – have formed a firm foundation for research, and also guide the development of cultural theory (Spillman 2016).

Three lenses on meaning-making processes

Cultural sociologists explore meaning-making processes based on these conceptual foundations. Given these foundations, what do you need to know to do cultural sociology? This book examines three lines of research in the field.

First, cultural sociologists focus on cultural objects and their properties. Unlike most other sociologists, they analyze in some depth what Berger and Luckmann called the "signs" mediating "the social construction of reality." For instance, how can different ways the same story is told generate different meanings? Or how does the weathering of billboards affect what they communicate? Rituals, symbols, evaluations, norms, and categories all express meaning through signs, and rather than taking this for granted, or assuming that signs can be ignored because they are transparent and simple, cultural sociologists consider how the cultural forms of signs influence processes of meaning-making. This is the most distinctive added value of cultural sociology compared to other perspectives in sociology.

Second, cultural sociologists analyze interaction as a meaning-making process. Frequently building on sociology's long interest in symbolic interaction, they focus on how interaction between individuals and within smaller groups influences meaning-making. For instance, how do childhood interactions create long-lasting musical or political tastes, and how do those tastes affect an individual's subsequent interactions and prospects? Or how do subcultures demonstrate their differences from the mainstream? Processes of action and interaction shape the expression and interpretation of the meaning of even widely shared signs.

Third, cultural sociologists analyze how culture is produced in large organizations, institutions, or fields of action. Frequently building on sociology's long interest in social structure and in large organizations, they focus on how meaning-making is influenced by large-scale patterns of social relations and organizational constraints. For instance, how does the mass production of music in large corporations affect the sort of music produced, compared to music performed in smaller and more informal settings? Or how does the pattern of relations among journalists, government officials, and non-profit providers all interested in humanitarian aid affect how mass violence is viewed? While any given individual may be unaware of the larger patterns of social relations affecting their meaning-making, cultural sociologists demonstrate many ways in which patterns of relations in the larger society are a critical influence on cultural production.

So cultural sociologists use three different lenses when they examine processes of meaning-making. They explore cultural forms, interaction, and the organization of production. The perspectives offered by these three angles of vision are irreducible, but compatible. Certainly, cultural theorists sometimes debate which lens is best, or question the significance of one aspect or another of meaning-making. As we will see, many investigations highlight one or another. However, since each lens offers different insights about culture, they can and often should be fruitfully combined for a fuller picture.

This framework is built primarily around concepts, rather than people. For this reason, it should be possible to follow it through to apply it flexibly to different authors, works, and research projects beyond those mentioned here. The overall schema can be used to think about different thematic emphases and significant authors, and to identify similarities and differences in different scholarly contexts, including different national contexts.

The critical element shared by all three approaches is their examination of processes of meaning-making. This focus distinguishes cultural sociology from other lines of investigation in sociology. Not only is culture irreducible to biology, as noted above, it is also irreducible to social structure, so sociological analysis with a restricted focus on large social structures and patterns of social relations (ignoring their meaning) is distinct from what cultural sociologists do. In the same way, cultural sociology is not restricted to a focus on individuals. That means that analysis centrally focused on individuals or individual processes, such as in social psychology, or even in the aggregations of individual opinions found in surveys, is not enough for cultural sociology. Instead, by establishing culture as a distinct level of analysis, not restricted to social structures or individuals, cultural sociology offers the advantage of linking social structures and individual subjectivity, which the earlier Berger and Luckmann concept of "the social construction of reality" also attempted.

These foundations have proven strong and the three angles of investigation highly productive for learning about culture from a sociological point of view (Alexander et al. 2012; Hall et al. 2010). The range of new knowledge cultural sociologists have produced is exciting; many examples will be offered in the following chapters.

This new knowledge about processes of meaning-making is important for several reasons. First, since meaning-making is important to everyone, understanding more about meaning, rather than sidelining it, should be important to sociologists. Second, understanding the meanings people share helps us understand how social groups cohere, and how complex social organization is accomplished. Third, understanding more about cultural difference offers important insights into how power and inequality are maintained. Fourth, understanding more about cultural conflict offers important insights into some of the most pressing social problems we face. To take a few recent examples, research in cultural sociology has shed light on bias in hiring processes, on health and aging, on environmental issues, and on processes of globalization.

Lauren Rivera expands on an important stream of cultural sociology which demonstrates how meaning-making processes affect inequality. She investigates how cultural assumptions influence the hiring process for elite jobs. Her observations and interviews show that bias was unconsciously imported into hiring decisions by employers' use of metrics and standards for qualities more accessible to candidates with more privileged backgrounds. Throughout the hiring process – in eligibility criteria, on-campus recruiting, interview training, résumé screening, face-to-face interviews, and hiring committee deliberations – she identifies ways in which the "seemingly economically neutral" decisions and measurements involved in the hiring process are in fact tied to cultural indicators and "pedigree." For example, interviewers worked with an informal criterion of "cultural fit" biased towards privileged experiences and lifestyle (Rivera 2015, 26–7, 3).

The topic of age and health may seem fundamentally biological, but Corey Abramson explores the cultural context of aging. His observations and interviews demonstrate, first, that, as we noted above, age stages are cultural categories: "old age" is a "cultural category with shared characteristics, challenges, expectations, and prejudices" which shape daily life (Abramson 2015, 10). But differences in cultural beliefs, motivations, and strategies also affect how people navigate old age. For instance, some people see their goal as bodily preservation, while others focus on maximizing enjoyment. Some people understand help from their social ties as a general obligation, while others see helping in terms of specific exchanges. Individuals' cultural resources are an important influence on how successfully they pursue their goals, too: for instance, how they navigate medical bureaucracies (Abramson 2015, 134, 143).

Justin Farrell investigates another topic which may initially seem irrelevant to culture: the environment. He explores processes of meaning-making about environmental protection, and their implications for environmental issues. His in-depth examination of persistent and interconnected conflicts surrounding Yellowstone, America's first and most iconic national park, suggests that the disputes among different stakeholders are generated by the different "socially constructed stories that give them meaning and direct their lives" – whether those stories are about, for example, rugged individualism, old-western heritage, indigenous religion, or the intrinsic value of non-human animals. Such stories create a moral and spiritual context for environmental disputes like those at Yellowstone, yet culture is so deeply ingrained that individuals often fail to recognize the influence of the moral culture within which they are embedded, or even to be able to give a coherent account of their beliefs and behaviors – "taken for granted as fundamental to reality" (Farrell 2015, 14, 9).

To take another example, globalization is necessarily a large-scale process which often seems to happen behind our backs and beyond daily life. Yet even so, examining meaning-making processes sheds new light on how economic globalization is expressed in intimate interactions and takes on different significance in different contexts. For instance, Kimberly Hoang's (2015) observations and interviews in four different Vietnamese hostess bars uncover links between macro-level flows of capital and trends in the informal economy around intimacy and gender performance. Hostesses in some bars oriented to elite Vietnamese businessmen, who want to display Vietnamese economic progress with conspicuous consumption and "Pan-Asian modernity," project expensiveness and Western-influenced standards of beauty, including lighter skin and rounder eyes. By contrast, hostesses in bars oriented to Westerners stick to an earlier type of gender performance, and with their darker skin tones, smoky eye makeup, and simple clothes they reinforce ideas of Western dominance by playing into images of an exotic Vietnam in need of aid.

Attentive to the rituals, symbols, evaluations, norms, and categories embedded in their research sites, these authors contribute significant new knowledge about topics of central concern to sociologists and the general public alike. By investigating the social construction of everyday life in hiring, old age, environmental conflict, and globalizing cities, they shed light on both consensus and conflict, solidarity and power. They analyze cultural forms, like the criteria for evaluation used by hiring companies, and the stories people tell about the environment. They analyze interaction processes, like the different ways old people engage with health providers, or the negotiations between women and their clients in Vietnamese bars. And they show how institutions, organizations, and fields – from hiring organizations to global financial flows – shape meaning-making processes.

Conclusion

How can we learn to understand culture better? How can we learn more about shared assumptions we take for granted, cultural differences which puzzle us, cultural power which affects us despite ourselves, and cultural conflict which frequently erupts in society?

The first step is to develop a reflective orientation to the culture surrounding us. Attention to *rituals, symbols, evaluations, norms,* and *categories* sensitizes us as observers to meaning-making we might otherwise take for granted. We also need to understand the historical ambiguities of the concept of culture. Remembering that, historically, the idea of culture was used to label two quite different things – *a separate realm of society, or a feature of entire groups* – helps guard against unnecessary confusion. Beginning to think of *culture as meaning-making process* is a way to encompass both historical senses, as well as the enormous variety of meaning-making we see in the world.

Against this background orientation, the remaining chapters in this book offer an extended answer to the question "what is cultural sociology?" by explaining and demonstrating many of the conceptual tools cultural sociologists now use to help us understand meaning-making better. What do you need to know to do cultural sociology? Each chapter will offer a different angle of vision on cultural processes and illustrate different conceptual tools for understanding culture. The following chapter examines how and why cultural sociologists analyze cultural forms. Chapter 3 surveys the various ways cultural sociologists examine meaning in interaction. In chapter 4, we explore larger-scale processes of organized cultural production. Against this background, chapter 5 provides a summary overview, sketches a critical assessment of this book using the tools of cultural sociology, demonstrates debates and differences among cultural sociologists, and suggests how to begin to use the conceptual tools of cultural sociology. Throughout, we see contributions to many general political and economic topics central to sociologists, such as inequality, identity politics, social movements, and organizations. We also see contributions to our knowledge of specialized cultural products like the arts, popular culture, religion, and science.

Sociology has come a long way in understanding "the social construction of reality" since Berger and Luckmann coined the term in the sixties. Building on many interdisciplinary influences, as well as the sociological classics, sociologists stopped marginalizing the idea of culture, and cultural research and theory boomed. It is time for a stock-taking of what we have learned and how we now understand meaning and meaning-making processes. The following chapter discusses the biggest innovation in sociological understanding of culture: the analysis of cultural forms and their independent influence on meaning-making processes.

2
Making Meaning Central

What do you need to know to do cultural sociology? First and most important, cultural sociologists interpret and analyze symbolic forms. As cultural sociologist Robin Wagner-Pacifici argues, "[I]t is only by gaining access to the operations and logics of the inner workings of cultural objects that any cultural sociology can begin to track the meanings and resonance of these objects in the social contexts in which they appear" (2010, 109). Before we examine meaning in interaction and the social organization of meaning-making, we need to understand how symbolic forms are themselves important influences in meaning-making processes, with intrinsic sociological interest. This chapter provides an overview of the major approaches cultural sociologists have adopted to analyzing cultural forms.

When, in 1966, Berger and Luckmann explained "the social construction of reality," they noted that everyday life was sustained by significations, signs clustered in systems which we encounter as objective and powerful: for instance, they noted, language "forces me into its patterns" and "typifies experiences" (1966, 38, 39). Mostly absent in sociology when they wrote were robust theoretical perspectives for analyzing signs as cultural structures. Signification processes were mostly ignored in favor of social organization, socialization, and action.

Cultural theorist and anthropologist Clifford Geertz noticed this blind spot in "Ideology as a Cultural System," one of several influential essays of his widely read by early cultural sociologists. Social scientists at the time, he said, lacked "anything more than the most rudimentary conception of the processes of symbolic formulation." This underestimated the power of the sign, the link between individual socialization and structured patterns of social relations, in Berger and Luckmann's "social construction of reality." As Geertz went on to say, "[T]he problem of how … ideologies transform sentiment into significance and so make it socially available is short-circuited" (1973, 207).

Just as Geertz observed, sociologists have often treated signs as transparent and inert, not worthy of independent analysis. Until quite recently, they have been more interested in the surrounding social context than the signs themselves. By contrast, scholars more attentive to language and imagery dig deeper into how signs work apart from the interactional or structural contexts which generate them. They observe, for instance, how the same facts can mean different things depending on whether they are put together in a tragic or romantic story. Or they might analyze how an image is created to symbolize rugged masculinity or deferential femininity.

What exactly is being neglected when social scientists neglect "processes of symbolic formulation"? French philosopher and literary critic Roland Barthes provided some popular illustrations of how to analyze the power of the sign in *Mythologies*, a collection of essays about popular culture originally published in the 1950s. For example, he analyzed wrestling as entertainment. Standard social science approaches might investigate how wrestlers train and interact with each other or their audience; or they might investigate how wrestling as entertainment industry is affected by larger social patterns like media markets, or class stigma. Barthes analyzed instead the conventional and structured signs of wrestling itself as a grandiloquent and detailed performance of good, evil, justice, suffering, and defeat. He supported his analysis with close attention to the ways these meanings were signified in exaggerated and stereotypical bodies, movements, and gestures. In another famous example, he analyzed a magazine cover image of a young black soldier saluting. This simple denotation, or "signifier," also carried a strong connotation, or "signified," of Frenchness and militarism. Combined, they yield a mythical sign – the "signification"–normalizing what Barthes describes as the idea "that France is a great Empire, that all her sons, without any color discrimination, faithfully serve under her flag, and there is no better answer to the detractors of an alleged colonialism than the zeal shown by this Negro in serving his so-called oppressors" (Barthes 1972 [1957], 115). Here, Barthes uncovers an example of the sort of processes of symbolic formation that Geertz called for. He does not take the meaning-making for granted, but shows how the symbol creates the representation of inclusion and normalizes an ideology (Aiello 2006).

More recently, asking questions about how symbolic forms influence meaning has been very productive for cultural sociologists interested in understanding and explaining meaning-making processes. Karen Cerulo (1998) provides a striking illustration in her research on how media stories about violence are told. Studying journalism, images, and speeches about violence, she found that stories varied according to whether they highlighted the victim or perpetrator first, and the order of telling affected whether the violence seemed criminal or justifiable. Varying the sequence of the grammatical elements in relation to each other changed the implicit meaning of the story, even though the same basic information was conveyed. Surprisingly, journalists she interviewed were unaware of this pattern: for them, it was taken-for-granted, implicit knowledge. Audiences in focus groups mostly went along with the interpretation of the incident implied by the sequencing in the news stories, although sometimes they did offer resistant readings. Cerulo shows in this study that attending to the form of signs – in this case, something as simple as sequencing and ordering of words – can unearth neglected influences on meaning-making processes.

Developing more precise and sophisticated analysis of intrinsic features of symbolic forms is the most distinctive contribution of cultural sociology compared to other sociological research. The following section summarizes intrinsic features of symbolic forms that are influential for meaning-making. The remainder of the chapter provides an overview of common approaches sociologists have used to analyze these features.

Convention, structure, and materiality in symbolic forms

How is meaning generated by symbolic forms? According to John Thompson, two often-forgotten features of signs that are important for generating significance are convention and structure (1990, 139–43). Subsequent theorists have added a third important condition of signification: its material forms.

First, signs are *conventional*, relying on rules, codes, or conventions (such as grammar, etiquette, or color coding) to convey meaning. Conventions may be deliberately adopted to communicate or persuade, as we might color a warning red rather than green, or use a particular format to write a clear business letter. Much more commonly, however, conventions exist as shared, tacit knowledge, rather than formal, explicit knowledge. Native speakers cannot formulate everything they say in conscious awareness of correct grammar; similarly, conventional knowledge about how to behave in a classroom, or the tone to adopt in a blog post, is almost always tacit. We usually notice conventions only when they are challenged. As we saw in chapter 1, norms are important elements of culture; conventions about how to use signs to convey meaning are an important type of widespread norm. The fact that the journalists Karen Cerulo interviewed were unaware of the sequencing patterns she discovered in news stories about violence shows how consequential tacit conventions can be. The capacity to recognize and analyze tacit social conventions producing meaning is a valuable skill for doing cultural sociology.

A number of contemporary sociological approaches to analyzing cultural forms discussed in this chapter offer ways of making explicit mostly tacit social conventions which make symbolic objects meaningful. First, they analyze *cognitive categories*. Then, attention to *symbolic boundaries* between categories or groups has been particularly productive for sociologists, especially those interested in inequality. Both categories and symbolic boundaries are elements of more complex social *schemas* or *frames* shaping common perceptions of the world. Evaluative relations between categories established in modern, rationalized societies have also been productively investigated as processes of *valuation* and *commensuration*. All these concepts identify symbolic forms and processes of meaning-making emergent from common social-psychological processes and are useful for the insights they offer into cultural conventions.

A second feature of signs which generates significance is that they are *structured*, "consisting of elements in determinant relations to each other" (Thompson 1990, 141), and these structured relations are crucial for generating meaning. The pronoun "I" gains its meaning through its implicit grammatical relation to "you" and "we": the grammatically structured relation makes meaning. And as Cerulo showed, different sequential structures in stories of violence can generate different meanings, even if they include all the same elements. Even more than conventions, the structured relations between symbolic elements are almost always a matter of implicit knowledge, and very much taken for granted in everyday life. However, they certainly influence meaning-making, as the example of stories of violence shows. The ability to recognize and analyze structured patterns of symbolic elements is another valuable skill for doing cultural sociology.

Some contemporary sociological approaches to cultural forms provide conceptual tools for analyzing how structured patterns of relations between signs influence meaning. These approaches begin by examining the "determinant relations" between cultural elements, not simply their conventional cognitive foundations. Overall, attention to discourse and *discursive fields* uncovers patterns in meaning-making which set boundaries on what can be said in particular circumstances. Within discourses, attention to *binary codes* helps us to analyze how fundamental conceptual contrasts provide a widespread, implicit grammar for communication among members of a group or society. Attention to *narrative* examines how events link together in a story, how identities are understood over time, and how the taken-for-granted emplotment of stories about events influences their interpretation. Attention to *genre* focuses on types of cultural objects, such as music, war memorials, or speeches, examining how they are formally distinguished, and the social implications of those formal distinctions.

Third, signs rely directly or indirectly on their material forms, which also affect possibilities of meaning-making. Meaning is stabilized in material forms, and the persistence and circulation of objects affect the accessibility of the meanings they convey to actors. Meanings of cultural objects may also change in unexpected ways as their material form changes. The ability to recognize and analyze the stabilizing and destabilizing impact of material forms for meaning-making is a third valuable skill for doing cultural sociology. Contemporary cultural sociologists are now developing conceptual tools for examining how the *materiality* of signs influences meaning-making in often unrecognized ways. Cultural sociologists are also analyzing the impact of material forms for cultural objects which generate conscious, often-intense recognition through their aesthetic power by approaching them as *icons*. The *iconic power* of some meaningful material objects is generated in part by the aesthetic effect of their material surface.

As this brief summary shows, some of the authors who investigate cultural forms and their social implications ground their analysis in the conventional features of symbols; sometimes, they connect conventions about symbols to psychological processes. Others focus in more depth on a special and particularly consequential class of conventions, the publicly available, structural features of signs in social context. A third group analyze how the material forms of signs influence meaning-making. Although each of these types of analytic tools has been developed from different intellectual roots and, to some extent, relies on different assumptions about appropriate foundations for cultural analysis, they have all proved flexible and illuminating when applied to a variety of sociological topics, and resulted in some of the most distinctive and innovative research in cultural sociology. Mostly, these different ways of understanding symbolic forms in more depth are compatible, and scholars will use them in various combinations. This in-depth analysis of signs is the most distinctive trait of cultural sociology compared to other approaches in sociology. And what distinguishes all these approaches to analyzing signs from other perspectives a cultural sociologist may adopt is a primary focus on how symbolic forms create meaning, rather than taking their meaning for granted.

Cognitive categories and symbolic boundaries

As psychologists and neuroscientists show, cognitive processes like learning, memory, perception, and attention are generic features of our capacities as humans. All these processes rely on categories and classification, and, as Émile Durkheim posited, classification is an essentially social process. According to Durkheim (1995 [1912]), the ways we perceive, evaluate, and act in our social environments, and even the ways we orient ourselves in time and space, emerge from our experience in our social groups. So one of the basic conceptual tools for analyzing culture is the concept of *cognitive categories*.

A classic example of such sociological analysis of cognitive categories is Durkheim's important argument that religions are constituted through the categories of "sacred" and "profane," which are defined in relation to each other (Durkheim 1995 [1912], 34). Mary Douglas's analysis of the category of "dirt" as "matter out of place ... the by-product of a systematic ordering and classification of matter, in so far as ordering involves rejecting inappropriate elements" (1966, 35), is another famous illustration. Around the time cultural sociology was emerging, Barry Schwartz continued this analytic tradition by exploring how and why a vocabulary of vertical classification (upper/lower, etc.) is linked in many different groups to evaluation of prestige and value (upper class, lower class, etc.). In his account, these widespread cognitive categories originate in the common experience of children comparing themselves to adults (Schwartz 1981, 109).

Some scholars interested in cognitive categories focus on the generic social-psychological and neuroscientific basis of humans' capacity to categorize (Adolphs 2009; see also DiMaggio 2002). Sociologists building on this line of inquiry draw attention to the practical grounding of common categories in common practices, as in Schwartz's account of vertical classification (see also Lizardo 2012). Others also explore general processes of cognition but focus less on the social-psychological preconditions and more on different ways the human capacity to categorize actually works in making meaning (Cerulo 2002). For instance, Eviatar Zerubavel focuses on the processes by which cognitive categories are marked or blurred, highlighted or bracketed, and how the same categories may operate differently in different times, places, and social locations. He argues that we need to go beyond individual psychological processes to look at the surrounding social context to understand categorization (Zerubavel 1991, 1997; Zerubavel and Smith 2010). Cognition is not simply in our heads but distributed across networked members of groups (Norton 2018a). And cultural sociology's attention to social variation in the content and operation of conventional cognitive categories can contribute to understanding important questions in cognitive psychology (Lamont et al. 2017).

So cultural sociologists have often examined and compared the different social conventions supporting common cognitive categories (Brekhus 2015). For example, while we all experience the passing of time, time has been measured and marked very differently in different societies (Zerubavel 1981). Other categories we often take for granted in modern life (though this was less the case in pre-modern societies) are "home" and "work." Christena Nippert-Eng (1996) shows how people define those categories in practice: for instance, whether they mix work with home life, or strictly separate the two, foreshadowing later research interest into how "spillover" from work to home and vice versa can affect quality of life.

In chapter 1, we saw that everyday categories which seem biologically obvious – such as the cognitive categories of childhood, adolescence, adulthood, and old age – are understood very differently in different groups at different times. More recently, cultural sociologists have been exploring how categories matter for the contemporary life course in other ways. For example, Jamie Mullaney (2001) argues that identities are often constructed negatively around rejected behaviors: she shows, for instance, how the category of "virgin" – a "never identity" – is constructed interactionally and biographically based on active choices regarding the surrounding society's moral code. Thomas DeGloma (2014), meanwhile, shows that some autobiographical accounts of personal development and change – "awakening" stories – make sharply distinct "before" and "after" categories in the storyteller's life.

Conventional cognitive categories shape our understanding of public settings, as well as personal life. Indeed, even the conventional categorization of "public" and "private" as separate spheres is socially constructed, shifting, and contentious (e.g. Nippert-Eng 2010; Okin 1989). And in contemporary public life, cultural sociologists have shown many important ways that conventional cognitive categories matter both in the economy and in politics.

In economic life, for example, Vanina Leschziner shows how the restaurant industry categories of food and cuisine bind "creativity in the kitchen and reputation in the marketplace." As she observes more generally, "Categories and classifications matter in any cultural endeavor and any economic market because they influence how creators understand their work, how arbiters assess it, and how consumers perceive it" (2015, 49, 50). Elsewhere I have also shown how businesses often collaborate in trade associations to "articulate, systematize and promote cognitive categories ... providing models for firms faced with uncertainty," like the Irrigation Association's categories of "Agricultural," "Turf/Landscape," and so on (Spillman 2012b, 118–19). And as we saw in chapter 1, industries face penalties for spanning market categories (Hsu et al. 2009; Zuckerman 2004).

In much the same way, conventional cognitive categories shape politics: we often use nationality labels when we encounter social difference; census categories support particular types of racial categorization in the United States (Mora 2014); and political loyalties are categorized in overarching terms of parties, even though particular policy preferences may be more complex (Kreiss 2018).

Cognitive categories generally work through implicit conventions, and this very taken-for-grantedness gives them great power. For instance, as influential cultural sociologist Pierre Bourdieu (1991) pointed out, symbolic power is generated in what he calls "official naming"– such as with titles and qualifications. But cognitive categories are also at the center of many public debates over their power. Often a challenge to "naturalized" cognitive categories will prompt larger political challenges. Such challenges to naturalized cognitive categories are foundational in the sociology of race and ethnicity: theories of racial formation and challenges to racism are premised on recognition of both the power and the conventionality of racial and ethnic categories (Lamont 1999; Omi and Winant 1994). So, too, is the challenging of naturalized categories central to many theories in the sociology of gender (e.g. Epstein 1988, 2007), and, more recently, of sexuality (e.g. Brekhus 2003; Waidzunas 2015). And conflicts and social movements surrounding nationality, citizenship, and immigration are premised on claims about highlighting or bracketing the cultural categories in which they are defined. Even official census categories implicitly or explicitly direct government power in people's lives, as Mara Loveman and her co-authors show in relation to racial categories in Brazil (Loveman et al. 2012), and G. Cristina Mora and Michael Rodríguez-Muñiz (2017) show in relation to racial categories in the US census. As a result, all these categories evoke mobilization and challenge from those who are affected. Indeed, many social movements involve a public challenge to conventional cognitive categories.

As sociologists who investigate cognitive categories all recognize, meaning-making with conventional cognitive categories necessarily involves drawing boundaries: such as those between adolescent and adult, home and work, "citizen" and "foreigner," or, in Leschziner's study of elite cuisine, classical and modernist techniques or Middle Eastern and New American styles (2015, 53, 57). All examine, in different ways, how the boundaries establishing conventional cognitive categories are established, shifted, and occasionally challenged in historical and interactional processes. This is the flip side of exploring how cognitive categories are important for meaning-making.

Focusing particularly on *symbolic boundaries*, Michèle Lamont's influential comparative research examines how different groups establish, mark, and evaluate status differences. For example, expanding on Bourdieu's work on cultural distinction, she found that upper-middle-class men drew three sorts of symbolic boundaries when they evaluated others: moral, socio-economic, and cultural. How exactly these boundaries were drawn varied: for instance, for American men, socio-economic boundaries were more important than cultural boundaries, and the opposite was true in France (Lamont 1992). Nevertheless, cultural boundaries of the sort

Bourdieu emphasized can still be significant in the United States: for example, Bethany Bryson (1996) found that well-educated people disproportionately disliked music associated with the less-educated, preferring, for instance, "anything but heavy metal." The study of symbolic boundaries establishing status has expanded to include, for example, working-class boundaries (Lamont 2000). And it offers new comparative insights about processes of stigmatization and discrimination, especially towards racialized groups (Lamont et al. 2016).

Research on symbolic boundaries also extends beyond questions of class, gender, and racial status and stigma (Lamont and Molnar 2002). For example, sociologists consider the symbolic boundaries between science and non-science (Gieryn 1983; Panofsky 2014) and between different forms of science (Gauchat and Andrews 2018). To take a different example, Tom Waidzunas (2015) investigates how boundaries between sexual categories are challenged in the "boundary work" of social movements and scientific debates drawing distinctions between "science" and disreputable "fringe sciences."

Schemas, frames, valuation, commensuration

Cultural sociologists also investigate symbolic forms which are more complex aggregations of categories and boundaries. Scaling up to this more aggregated type of conventional symbolic form helps us understand more about the ways meaning-making in real settings interweaves different sorts of categories and boundaries. Many sociologists think of *schemas* as these complex symbolic forms which might include "not only ... the array of binary oppositions that make up a given society's fundamental tools of thought, but also the various conventions, recipes, scenarios, principles of action, and habits of speech and gesture built up with these fundamental tools" (Sewell 1992, 8). Schemas are "a distinct and strongly-interconnected pattern of interpretive elements [which] can be activated by minimal inputs ... an interpretation which is frequent, well organized, memorable" (D'Andrade 1992, 29). They are templates for understanding common social settings and problems, and may be actively transposed to make sense of new settings and problems. Schemas may assemble categories and boundaries deeply embedded in society, like "female and male, nature and culture, private and public," but also more complex templates for social life, like "rules of etiquette, or aesthetic norms, or such recipes for group action as the royal progress ... or the democratic vote" (Sewell 1992, 8).

For example, Mary Blair-Loy investigated a common social problem – work/family conflict – as a clash of two cultural schemas. For her, schemas are "shared cultural models we employ to make sense of the world" and "evoke intense moral and emotional commitment" (2003, 3). She compares the "family devotion schema" and "work devotion schema." In addition to being gendered, these schemas specify different views of what makes life meaningful, and what is rewarding. So these schemas are built by association from a number of different categories and boundaries. And Blair-Loy shows they have normative force: even when female finance executives earned very high salaries, and economic rationality suggested that their male partners should shoulder the domestic role, many couples found it difficult to violate these shared normative schemas, and some did not even consider doing so.

Many sociologists think of schemas in terms of the similar idea of "*frames*," a concept introduced to sociology by Erving Goffman (2010 [1974]). Some cultural sociologists have recently suggested that we should reserve the concept of "schemas" for personal, simple, unconscious cultural forms (much like the cognitive categories "up" and "down" mentioned above) and think of "frames" as public symbolic forms (Wood et al. 2018). Frame analysis was promoted especially by sociologists studying social movements (Snow et al. 2014), who found the concept a useful way of analyzing cultural forms which might encourage political challenge. When social movement challengers adopt frames, they are often – though not always – deliberate and strategic in their choice of how to present their issue, to encourage supporters and persuade the public. For example, as Deanna Rohlinger notes in her study of abortion politics in the United States, "generally speaking, framing an issue in a way that is amenable to organizational goals is a constant challenge with which a group must contend" (2015, 8–9). Similarly, in a study of opposing social movements – ex-gay and gay rights – promoting and challenging the scientific validity of "reparative therapy" for gay men, Waidzunas (2015) demonstrates how framing and counterframing can mutually shape the messaging and tone of the opposing groups, and identifies frame disputes *within* movements as well. In examples like these, the concept of frames connotes elements of consciousness and strategy which the concept of schemas does not. However, it is important to note that complex symbolic forms – concatenations of simpler categories and boundaries – are not all deliberately formulated in this way, but sometimes function more like a common language, situating actors in a broader field.

Beyond the study of social movements, cultural sociologists have investigated many other forms of public culture as frames. For example, Rodney Benson (2013) analyzed media coverage of immigration news in France and the United States across four decades and identified frames which are still easily recognized and persistent today. Six frames portrayed immigrants in a positive light: as victims of the global economy, humanitarian crisis, or xenophobia, and as heroes contributing cultural diversity, social integration, and useful work. Four frames he identified characterized immigrants as a threat: to jobs, to public order, to the cost of public services, and to national cohesion. He found, for example, that whereas, overall, American media tended to stress "individualist, market-oriented frames" – threats to jobs and public costs, and immigrants as good workers – French media tended to stress "civic solidarity" frames such as threats to national cohesion. The frames Benson analyzes constitute widely available, often taken-for-granted symbolic forms which generate "selective perception" (2013, 19, 4).

Schemas and frames sometimes encapsulate the forms in which we perceive the world in ways which seem quite neutral, in the sense that everyone within a group sharing those cultural forms would commonly find it difficult to see things differently, or to communicate in different terms. Sociologists, though, have been particularly interested in the ways that schemas and frames additionally express and reinforce value judgements, and they have turned a critical lens on their ideological implications. Many sociologists interested in *(e)valuation* focus on how the assemblage of categories and boundaries in schemas and frames expresses widely shared value judgements and imposes hierarchy. As Lamont (2012) shows, valuation and evaluation rely on processes of categorization and legitimation which are central concerns of cultural sociology. Comparative analysis of these processes shows, for example, different ways that the stigmatization of subordinate groups is experienced (Lamont et al. 2016), different ways that environmental issues are evaluated (Espeland 1998; Fourcade 2011), and different ways that economic exchanges are made (Zelizer 1983). In their influential theory of valuation, Luc Boltanski and Laurent Thévenot (2006 [1991]) identify six very different principles by which evaluations may be made, among them industrial logic (productivity), domestic logic (interpersonal relations), and civic logic (collective unity). Evaluations of the same object may be very different according to the principles – the schemas or frames – which are used.

Meaning-making processes of evaluation may often be implicit and informal, and all the more effective for that. We may not even recognize that we are judging – or stigmatizing – when we use some evaluative schemas and frames. In modern life, however, processes of evaluation are often explicitly formalized in ubiquitous and influential ratings and rankings. *Commensuration* – the deliberate representation and evaluation of different units with a common metric – changes what might otherwise be seen as complex qualitative differences into quantitative relations (Espeland and Stevens 1998). Commensuration processes like bestseller lists, college rankings, and standardized tests vary in their complexity, but many involve elaborate and formal meaning-making processes, including the explicit creation of comparable categories and boundaries. They often affect subsequent behavior – such as in "teaching to the test" – and develop authority and legitimacy even despite the common recognition of qualitative differences that are not captured in ratings and rankings (Espeland and Stevens 2008; see also Berman and Hirschman 2018; Fourcade 2016).

Analyzing schemas, frames, valuation, and commensuration, cultural sociologists are able to focus on more complex symbolic forms assembled from a variety of cognitive categories and boundaries. They expand and deepen our understanding of the social conventions which make meaning.

Discursive fields, binary codes, narratives, and genres

Another important set of approaches to analyzing symbolic forms focuses particularly on their internal structures. There is more to symbolic forms than convention. As Thompson pointed out, symbolic structures are also essential for meaning-making. These structures are emergent properties of culture. If we only think of symbolic forms as conventional, and ignore their structuring, the ad hoc empirical proliferation of different sorts of categories – boundaries, schemas, frames, and icons – across society seems random, and it is hard to understand long-term cultural persistence and structural pressures on cultural change (Norton 2014b).

A cultural structure consists of "elements which stand in determinate relations with each other," and in analyzing the structure of symbolic forms, we "analyze the specific elements and their interrelations" (Thompson 1990, 141). Just as linguist Ferdinand Saussure (1990 [1916]) distinguished between language (as a general system) and speech (as particular instances of that system), many cultural sociologists analyze relations between symbolic elements in particular discourses to show how they instantiate broader cultural patterns, "languages," which help us understand meaning-making across many different settings. As Jeffrey Alexander and Philip Smith noted in an influential argument for the sociological significance of cultural structures, "[W]hen they are interrelated, symbols provide a nonmaterial structure. They represent a level of organization that patterns action as surely as structures of a more visible, material kind" (1993, 156).

At the most general level, sociologists interested in cultural structures examine discourses or discursive fields. Discourses are complex cultural forms which include all the various ways meaning is articulated around a particular topic of investigation: "[S]ign sets are organized into discourses" (Alexander and Smith 1993, 157). Discourses may include not only linguistic forms of various sorts – conversations, narratives, speeches, newsletters, official reports, journalism, etc. – but also non-linguistic elements like images, rituals, and monuments. Sometimes, discourse analysis focuses on a singular cultural thread unified around one point of view. For instance, Ruth Braunstein (2018) analyzes a discourse of Christian nationalism and religious exclusion evident in American history, but often overshadowed by more "civic" discourses about freedom and inclusion she also explores elsewhere.

More often, however, sociologists analyze wider arrays of meaning-making incorporating different perspectives on a topic. *Discursive fields* "offer a space or field within which discourse can be framed" (Wuthnow 1989, 555). They are cultural structures within which a variety of potentially conflicting points of view are articulated. Importantly, discursive fields also set limits on what meaning-making can make sense in a given context (Spillman 1995), filtering the power of macro-social context in smaller-scale interaction. For example, claims about the meaning of national identity may be expressed in many ways: focusing, for instance, on political symbols, historical events, the land, or religion, among many other possibilities. But these symbolic forms make sense as claims about national identity only if they are connected to the discursive field which structures national identity. They must be plausible ways of expressing either shared qualities across internal population difference or claims about relations with other nations (Spillman 1997, 136–50). A wide variety of potentially conflicting points of view on national identity may be articulated, and themes within the discursive field will vary according to time and group context, but if a symbol does not support claims about internal commonality or place in the world, it will not make sense as a claim about national identity. The discursive field limits meaning-making possibilities. Unlike in the nineteenth century, when some Americans and many Australians claimed shared "Anglo" inheritance, it would now sound like a grammatical error to claim that what Americans or Australians share is common ethnic descent (as the Japanese might continue to do). This is true even though other claims, like Australians' connection to the land, are just as imaginary. Now, claiming common ethnic descent as a central feature of Australian or American national identity would be "ungrammatical" in the discursive field constituting national identity because it could not support claims about internal commonality across social difference (Spillman 1997).

Sociologists interested in analyzing discursive fields have tackled many of the big issues confronting society, offering new understanding of large-scale, historically persistent meaning-making within constraining frameworks which yet encompass multiple viewpoints, and based on large sets of linguistic and non-linguistic symbolic forms. For example, Ronald Jacobs and Eleanor Townsley (2011) analyze and explain a distinct discursive field, "the space of opinion," including political columnists and television pundits, with a cultural logic and history distinct from related fields of journalism and politics. They argue that it is an important but understudied feature of the public sphere and democratic politics, and investigate its history, participants, formats, and rhetoric in the United States. They provide an intriguing foundation for exploring recent changes in the space of opinion with the growing influence of social media.

Some discursive fields may be transnational. For example, John Hall (2016) analyzes the discursive field associated with global climate change, showing how different perspectives are based on different understandings of the future. To take another example, Joachim Savelsberg (2015) examined how different groups of transnational professionals understood the mass violence and human rights violations in Darfur in the early years of this century. International lawyers framed the violence and human rights violations as a matter of crime and justice; international aid organizations framed them as a humanitarian catastrophe (downplaying blame); and diplomats also bracketed justice concerns, understanding the problem with a focus on achieving substantive peace. Taken together, and as journalists channeled these sources, the different frames constituted a discursive field surrounding the

Darfur atrocities. However, even given the variety of possible frames, the structure of this discursive field excludes the possibility that the violence could be claimed to be legitimate (as Cerulo [1998] showed in some media stories of violence).

Discourse analysis may focus generally on recurrent themes or topics or ways of understanding which, taken in relation to each other, make up the range of ways that a shared concern may be understood (and debated) across different social contexts. Within discursive fields, particular themes may be analyzed as schemas (as in Blair-Loy's findings about work–life balance) or as frames (as Savelsberg labels the different perspectives on the Darfur crisis). Going beyond this looser approach, cultural sociologists also offer a more technically precise way of analyzing discursive fields. Taking a cue from Durkheim's argument that the categorical opposition between sacred and profane constitutes religion (regardless of the myriad particular things which religions might label as sacred or profane), many contemporary discourse analysts in sociology identify persistent *binary codes* which constitute structural foundations for meaning-making within discursive fields. These codes are arrays of simple categorical oppositions which, taken together, provide tools for meaning-making.

In one of the most well-known studies introducing and developing discourse analysis based on binary codes, Alexander and Smith (1993) analyze political discourse in the United States. Claims-making in American politics is always based on a set of symbolic oppositions constituting the "democratic/counter-democratic code." For example, institutions may be labeled impersonal or personal, rule-regulated or arbitrary, inclusive or exclusive, and so forth. Similarly, social relationships may be labeled open or secret, truthful or deceitful, etc. And people may be characterized as active or passive, reasonable or hysterical, and realistic or unrealistic. In the rough and tumble of politics, people, relationships, and institutions are labeled and relabeled in attempts at persuasive claims-making. Alexander and Smith find the same cultural "grammar" operating as politicians debate many controversial issues – used by speakers on opposite sides, and evident as much in debates from the early nineteenth century that we now have a hard time understanding as it is in more recent political debates. Subsequent research has shown the same democratic/anti-democratic code structuring claims-making in electoral campaigns (Alexander 2010; Norton 2018b) and important social movements for political inclusion – including the feminist movements and the civil rights movement (Alexander 2006). Of course, as this perspective also emphasizes, creative action and organizational resources are also essential for the outcomes of political claims-making structured by binary codes. But discourse structured in terms of these foundational, persistent binary codes is a fundamental condition of American politics. Cultural sociologists interested in binary codes are now tracing similarities and differences in the language of politics beyond the United States – in Latin America, East Asia, and elsewhere (Alexander and Tognato 2018; Alexander et al. 2019a, 2019b). For example, Hee-Jeong Lee (2018) shows how a national South Korean debate about identification cards combined claims based on the democratic code with claims based on a developmental code sacralizing efficiency, productivity, convenience, and so on.

Analysis of discourse structure in terms of binary codes emergent in claims-making is sometimes wrongly understood to imply consensus: for instance, that members of a group all share the same political opinions. Nothing could be further from the truth. What a discursive structure like the binary code of civil society constitutes is not consensus, but the possibility of making understandable claims from very different points of view. Both conflict and consensus are only possible within shared discursive fields. The opposite of the binary code of civil society is not conflict, but claims-making that is irrelevant or incomprehensible.

This sort of "structuralist hermeneutics" – exploring the binary codes constituting the grammar of discursive fields for deeper and more generalizable understanding – has also been adopted to analyze meaning-making about a variety of other topics. For example, Klaus Weber, Kathryn Heinze, and Michaela DeSoucey (2008) show how activists and producers created a new market in grass-fed beef and dairy by mobilizing binary codes associated with authenticity (authentic/manipulated, honest/deceitful, connected/disconnected, etc.), sustainability (sustainable/exploitative, etc.), and nature (natural/artificial, etc.). Answering a very different question – what explains the under-utilization of condoms for health in sub-Saharan Africa? – Iddo Tavory and Ann Swidler (2009) show that understanding of the health benefits of condoms for AIDS prevention is complicated by specific semiotics associated with protected sex, such as trust versus distrust in love, or the perceived risk of condoms versus the risk of AIDS.

Binary code analysis identifies fundamental categorical oppositions generating meaning. How they are used in the real world can shift – for instance, a politician may be praised as rational or criticized as irrational by different people at different times – but the binary codes, as cultural structures, are static. Indeed, their fixity is an important feature, allowing analysts to generalize across many different processes of meaning-making. By contrast, a second set of more technically precise concepts for analyzing discourses draws on theories of *narrative* to help us analyze the ways stories are structured over time.

Narrative forms offer frameworks for accounts of temporal processes, capturing the ways action flows in linked events, and tell stories about action with a beginning, middle, and end. Narrative forms label heroes and anti-heroes, and fit their actions into common templates, such as tragedy, comedy, and romance. Narrators select personal or collective events and features which may be quite disparate, and emplot them within larger stories to make sense of them. Narrative meaning emerges from structuration, the connections made between different actions and events.

Cultural sociologists have shown that the importance of narrative form is not confined to fiction, the latest bestseller or popular movie. Meaning-making processes in the real world often rely on narrative form to make sense of identities and events, and differing narrations may compete within discursive fields (Polletta et al. 2011). For instance, in a prescient study of media accounts of the police beating of a black motorist, Ronald Jacobs (1996) shows how mainstream and African American news sources both developed tragic and romantic narratives about the event and its aftermath. However, their narratives were plotted differently, with different heroes: mainstream sources made civic leaders attempting police reform the heroes of a romantic narrative of public redemption; African American sources situated the event in a longer history of racial violence, and the African American community was the heroic actor battling for justice. Here, narrative analysis becomes a means of comparing variant interpretations within the same broader discursive field. In another illuminating study of narrative structure in meaning-making about public events, Philip Smith (2005) argues that mobilization for war in democratic societies requires an apocalyptic narrative pitting an "us" against a "them" who threaten our destruction. By contrast, more nuanced tragic narratives do not sustain the massive efforts necessary for war. And increasing scholarly attention is devoted to the ways in which narrative influences public policies, such as health policy regarding autism, and cultural policy for Europe (Beresford and Bullard 2018).

Cultural sociologists have also explored how narrative forms are used in critical social movements. Francesca Polletta (1998) argues that narratives differ from simpler "frames" because of the emplotment or connection between events, the multiple points of view, and the stock of familiar plot lines that they entail. Narratives, she argues, are particularly useful for social movements for articulating accounts of origins, such as, in the case of the civil rights movement, Rosa Parks' refusal to move to the back of a segregated bus. Narratives of defeat may also help sustain movements in difficult times, and, conversely, narratives can provide connections when movement goals succeed in entering institutionalized politics, such as when African American politicians laid claim to civil rights movement projects as they subsequently entered Congress. For Anne Kane (2000, 2011), the narratives used during another social movement – the Land War of Irish tenant farmers against the British (1879–82) – have a similar importance: "[T]hrough the sharing and contention over narratives regarding their history, their current situation, important contingent events, and their future, the Irish constructed a new master political narrative" (2000, 318).

A general focus on investigating discursive fields and a more specific analysis of binary codes or narratives offer different ways of investigating cultural structures. Sociologists have also adopted from the humanities the concept of *genre*, which identifies the formal or structural features which differentiate different established types of cultural forms. Cultural objects often "share conventions of form or content" which enable observers to classify them together as the same genre (DiMaggio 1987, 441; see also Griswold 1987). While the concept originally applied to artworks – types of novels, or types of drama, for example – it is equally useful as a way of characterizing similar conventional structure across a range of other cultural objects – types of video games, types of news story, and so on. Sociologists also highlight how social relations among producers of cultural objects and their audiences enable, constrain, and change genre conventions.

For example, Jennifer Lena includes both formal and social qualities in her extended study of different genre communities in popular music, defining musical genres as "systems of orientations, expectations, and conventions that bind together industry, performers, critics and fans in making what they identify as a distinctive sort of music" (2012, 6). Fundamental to her extended investigation of the organization of different types of genre communities, though, is the characterization of formal genre qualities which make musical styles distinct (even if the boundaries between them are low in periods of innovation). As she summarizes, for example, rap "is rhythmic, electronically based music combined with spoken, rhyming lyrics and sometimes sung choruses" whereas bluegrass "is characterized by the harmonizing sounds of the banjo, fiddle, and mandolin, with bass and guitar providing rhythmic accompaniment and the notable absence of drums, bass, woodwind, or electrified instruments" (2012, 28). By identifying genre forms, she is then able to examine how producers and consumers of music generate and change musical genres. Similarly, as we shall see below, the established genre of heroic war memorials became "a genre problem" after the problems associated with the Vietnam War in the United States, and innovation in the cultural form emerged as a resolution of that problem (Wagner-Pacifici and Schwartz 1991).

Materiality and iconicity

Symbolic forms are usually expressed in cultural objects. Cultural objects are also necessarily material. For example, symbols like flags often have strict material specifications and requirements. Rituals like the Olympic opening ceremony, with national teams marching behind their flags, rely for their power on technology for easily carrying flagpoles, and spatial design allowing both parading and mass assembly. Norms about raising the flag, or lowering it to half-mast, also rely on material design to be enacted smoothly. Evaluations may rely on material symbols, as when controversy erupts about whether a politician wears a flag pin, or about an artist's critical use of flag imagery. Cognitive categories and boundaries defining nations are represented by flags: different parties to international talks will each be represented by their flag, and national borders will be lined with flags. And the flag as an icon can evoke transcendent attachment in the mass spectacle of fireworks or sports. Even virtual cultural objects – a screensaver representing the flag, a video artist's rendition of flags flying across the country – rely on vast material infrastructure supporting our access. So another way of analyzing the impact of cultural forms focuses on their *materiality*.

As cultural sociologists interested in materiality point out, material form is not usually a trivial condition of meaning-making. Variations in material form influence processes of meaning-making. Material form can be consequential for meaning-making in at least two ways. First, it stabilizes meanings and memory. Not only are objects crucial for communication and self-expression – such as when consumption expresses social status (Bourdieu 1984) or when clothing or drinks symbolize different experiential realms (Nippert-Eng 1996) – but particular material qualities of objects affect possibilities of action and interaction (McDonnell 2010), sometimes over long periods (Gieryn 2002; Mukerji 2009). The distribution and circulation of material objects representing cognitive categories and cultural structures make those meanings accessible to us, and minimal distribution and circulation – lessening "retrievability" of meaning (Schudson 1989) – makes some meanings less accessible. Meaning materialized in objects also preserves and distributes cognition: we do not need to be conscious of all the culture we know all the time, in part because meanings are preserved in external objects and environments, which act as implicit reminders. From flags and church altars to wedding photos and calendars, material objects stabilize and preserve meanings, and allow us to take them for granted most of the time.

Conversely, material changes may destabilize meaning-making possibilities. Memories are lost when photo or recording technology changes. When billboards decay, their message changes too (McDonnell 2016). Promoters of new political ideals challenge older material symbols in the process of new meaning-making (Zubrzycki 2013). Activists challenge the preservation of statues of former heroes – such as Confederate generals in the American South, or communist founders in post-Soviet Russia – because taking them down would remove from common experience the implicit endorsement of political projects they represent.

Most often, the materiality of cultural objects influences meaning-making "behind our backs," preserving or undermining symbolic forms in ways that are all the more effective because they are implicit. Sometimes, though, material forms make a more demanding impact, explicitly and intensely generating attachment, with material surfaces possessing aesthetic and emotional power which is connected with, but not reducible to, deeper discursive and verbal meaning. Non-verbal, material, aesthetic qualities of some material objects – artworks, certainly, but many elements of popular culture too, especially in advertising – make them *icons*. Far from being restricted to religious settings, material objects with aesthetic qualities which attract explicit and intense meaning-making beyond the verbal or discursive level proliferate in contemporary society. *Iconic power* derives from a "mutually constitutive relation" between aesthetic surface and discursive depth (Bartmanski and Alexander 2012, 4). Iconicity emerges in the compression of meaning through the aesthetic experience of material objects. For example, some visual images of war and protest become iconic; some brands and celebrities exert iconic power; some buildings and artworks derive iconic power from the interaction between their surface aesthetics as material objects and the cognitive and moral meanings they may also represent. Iconicity may stabilize existing meaning – the Sydney Harbour Bridge and the Sydney Opera House become persistent representations of the city – but the power of icons may also destabilize, encouraging or implementing new forms of meaning making – as innovative architecture like the Burj Khalifa in Dubai makes a claim to global pre-eminence for the Middle East. And the loss of iconic material objects can be experienced as cultural trauma (Debs 2013).

The many ways that materiality and iconicity may be influential in meaning-making are evident in the story of the Vietnam Veterans Memorial, dedicated in Washington, DC, in 1982. As Robin Wagner-Pacifici and Barry Schwartz (1991) discuss in an influential early study of this national icon, the low-lying, somber, reflective black wall, simply inscribed with the names of dead soldiers shorn of rank or other heroic detail, was a radical innovation in memorial design. War memorials had previously stabilized the imputed, public, meaning of war in heroic form, in grand statues of swashbuckling generals on horseback, and lists of names surrounded by patriotic symbols. Glorious memories of war had been highlighted, made accessible, and stabilized in this taken-for-granted way for centuries. This sort of stabilization became very evident when it was challenged. The Vietnam War had been so unpopular and contentious that the public remained highly divided about whether, let alone how, to commemorate the dead. This controversy generated the innovative design, criticized by some as an inadequate commemoration of the soldiers' heroism, but embraced by many more as morally engrossing, drawing each viewer closer. The design destabilizes the possibility of traditional, heroic narratives of war, and stabilizes a new meaning: "honor the soldier, not the war." The memorial became iconic, a surface which draws the observer in to the moral meaning of the seemingly endless lists of names of the dead.

Conclusion

Interpretation of symbolic forms is central to cultural sociology. In contrast to other sociological perspectives, cultural sociology does not take cultural forms for granted, but examines "landscapes of meaning" (Reed 2011, 109) and the varying influence of the properties of signs themselves. Convention and structure make signs meaningful, and the material forms they take influence the possibilities and limits of meaning-making. Conversely, unfamiliar conventions, foreign cultural structures, and destabilized material forms will generate misunderstandings, puzzles, or meaninglessness.

Cultural sociology offers a range of conceptual tools with which to analyze symbolic forms. Many cultural sociologists have shown how identifying cognitive categories and symbolic boundaries helps us to understand unfamiliar others, identify what groups share, clarify cultural differences, and explain social conflict. Similar payoffs accrue to those who analyze more complex assemblages of categories and boundaries in schemas, frames, valuation, and commensuration.

One important type of cultural convention involves longstanding, historically persistent cultural forms which influence meaning-making of all sorts, across many different social contexts. These cultural structures may be analyzed generally as discursive fields, which establish the range and limits of viable claims-making about a topic in any given historical context, and with more technical precision in terms of binary codes and narrative form. Cultural sociologists also attend to the formal boundaries delineating cultural objects which are established by genre constraints. Exploring these cultural structures helps us understand shared patterns underlying apparent cultural particularity and incoherence, helps explain how cultural difference is generated, and helps account for the forms taken by persistent cultural conflicts.

The infrastructure of symbolic forms is also necessarily material, and examining how materiality may shape meaning-making can also help us understand more about shared meanings and cultural difference. Just like conventions and cultural structures, existing material forms may constrain and enable possibilities of meaning-making. One influential way material form may affect meaning-making is through icons and iconic power.

Decades ago, when Berger and Luckmann examined human meaning-making as the social construction of reality, sociology offered only an impoverished vocabulary for analyzing symbolic forms. Since then, an array of important concepts have been developed and demonstrated, offering different ways of grasping how symbolic forms constrain and enable meaning-making. Cultural analysis using ideas about cognitive categories, symbolic boundaries, schemas, frames, valuation, commensuration, discursive fields, binary codes, narratives, genre, material affordances, and iconicity offers ways of understanding the independent influence of symbolic forms and the role of convention and structure in meaning-making.

These different conceptual tools originated in somewhat different interdisciplinary influences and intellectual genealogies, including cognitive psychology, semiotics, literary criticism, and anthropology, and subsequently developed to apply to sociological questions and topics. Nevertheless, there is nothing fundamentally contradictory about drawing on these different tools in different ways, as long as we recognize that convention, structure, and materiality are all important features of symbolic forms. In any research project, the choice of conceptual approach will likely rest in part on the object of investigation.

This chapter has shown how cultural sociology expands our ability to attend to and analyze convention, structure, and materiality in meaning-making. However, as John Thompson (1990, 138–45) points out, meaning-making also relies on intentionality ("intentional expressions of a subject, or perceived as such by receivers or audiences"), reference ("expressing something beyond the sign itself"), and context ("embedded in specific social processes of production and reception"). Cultural sociologists draw on and develop established sociological theories for analyzing interaction and social structure to address these features of meaning-making. The next chapter explores sociological approaches to culture in action, which expand on the place of intentionality and reference as intrinsic features of meaning-making.

3
Meaning and Interaction

What do you need to know to do cultural sociology? We have already seen that cultural sociologists examine how convention and structure in symbolic forms influence meaning-making. In doing so, they think in terms of *cognitive categories*, *symbolic boundaries*, *schemas*, *frames*, *valuations*, *commensuration*, *discursive fields*, *binary codes*, *narratives*, *genres*, *materiality*, and *iconicity*. A second important skill involves examining how meaning-making proceeds in interaction. What does meaning-making in action look like, and how does interactional context shape meaning-making? To understand how meaning-making works in practice, we need to examine processes of interaction and taken-for-granted social contexts. For help in exploring this dimension of culture, cultural sociologists draw on sociology's longstanding theories of micro-social processes – of practices, situated action and interaction – especially the intellectual tradition of symbolic interactionism.

Action and interaction played an important part in Berger and Luckmann's influential account of "the social construction of reality." As they pointed out, "[A]ll symbolic universes and all legitimations are human products; their existence has its base in the lives of concrete individuals" (1966, 128). They analyzed the subjective reality of culture as a process of internalization through socialization. There are two types of socialization: fundamental, emotionally powerful, primary

socialization; and the "role-specific knowledge" – the vocabularies, tacit knowledge, legitimations, and ritual – embedded
in later, secondary socialization. For Berger and Luckmann,
this subjective dimension of meaning-making is sustained by
routines and everyday interaction. Everyday conversation
reaffirms and tweaks linguistic objectification of cultural
forms (1966, 138–9, 149, 153).

So, for example, we saw in the previous chapter that
Barthes' (1972 [1957]) famous analysis of wrestling focused
on the conventional and structured significations a match
conveyed. If you are interested in action and interaction, you
would then want to know more. How are wrestlers socialized
to perform? How do basic signs vary in different interaction
contexts? And how do different audiences interpret differently
the signs expressed in the match? Given the conventional
and structured sets of significations in wrestling, what then
happens with them in interaction?

Asking questions about meaning-making in interaction has
generated many important studies revealing the subjective
experience of meaning-making in a vast range of different
situations and settings. To take one example, Scott Jacques
and Richard Wright (2015) investigated the world of middle-
class, suburban teenage drug dealers – their motivations and
interactions with suppliers, customers, police, and parents.
They find many ways this world differed from that of poorer,
inner-city dealers, who are closer to the public stereotype of
drug dealers. For example, poorer dealers interacted combat-
ively as an essential deterrent to their own victimization
by suppliers, buyers, and police, and so violent encounters
were quite common. In contrast, for the suburban dealers,
who faced little victimization or attention from the police,
combativeness did not signify that dealers were protective
or cool. In one rare instance of fighting observed by Jacques
and Wright, a confrontation ran out of steam because of
"the cultural commitments that shaped day-to-day social
interaction" in the suburb. The authors trace in detail how
processes of interaction which might otherwise be conflictual
are muted by "the code of the suburb" rather than the "code
of the street" because of the privilege of their more protected
setting (Jacques and Wright 2015, 154–9; see also Anderson
1999; Duck 2015). Examining interaction closely, they

illuminate subjective meaning-making about drug-dealing which runs counter to contemporary assumptions based on research in very different settings. In doing so, they highlight in unexpected ways a chronic story of power and inequality.

Many such studies of meaning-making "on the ground" build on longstanding traditions of ethnography in qualitative sociology with roots in the Chicago School and symbolic interactionism. Cultural sociologists have incorporated these scholarly traditions, while also developing them. Whereas the earlier traditions always examined meaning-making processes by analyzing interaction, more recent developments in cultural sociology often go further, connecting observations about interaction processes to shared cultural forms. How are shared cultural forms – categories, boundaries, schemas, frames, evaluations, commensurations, discursive fields, codes, narratives, genres, materiality, and icons – incorporated, expressed, and altered in processes of interaction? What shared norms of interaction are themselves cultural forms transposable across different local settings?

In this chapter, we focus on the conceptual tools sociologists have used to analyze culture in processes of action and interaction.

Intention and reference in processes of meaning-making

Why do interaction processes affect meaning-making? Why is it sometimes insufficient to examine shared symbolic forms? We saw in the previous chapter that convention and structure are essential features of symbolic forms. Two other essential features of symbolic forms are intentionality and reference. These features anchor meaning-making in situated action contexts and capture how it is subjectively experienced. Symbolic forms are always expressions of and for a person or group: some level of intentionality is essential. Symbolic forms are also referential, linking to "a specific object or objects, individual or individuals, state of affairs or states of affairs" (Thompson 1990, 138, 143). Like intentionality, referentiality anchors symbolic forms in immediate subjective experience. In everyday life, what people are trying to say and what they are referring to with symbolic forms are the main features we are concerned with when we encounter them. These capture the subjective experience of meaning-making.

Intentions and references are always specific to interactional contexts. Unlike convention and structure, which transcend specific situations and different settings, intention and reference do not make sense outside of their practical interactional context. Cultural sociologists interested in meaning-making in action offer many ways of analyzing how specific social contexts pattern meaning-makers' use of symbolic forms to express intentions and make references.

Some sociological investigations of interactional contexts focus specifically on offering interpretations of very particular social contexts and situations. They add to our sociological knowledge by "giving voice" to otherwise ignored or misunderstood groups (Ragin and Amoroso 2019, 40–2). As Clifford Geertz once affirmed, including the meaning-making of different others in "the consultable record of what man has said" is an important contribution of social sciences (1973, 30). This research helps us better understand the worldviews of people who might be foreign to us, by delving into how their intentions and references make sense in context, even though they might initially be puzzling to outsiders. One of the great delights of cultural sociology is learning about different social worlds we would otherwise be unlikely to encounter. And adding to scholarly knowledge of different groups always helps challenge generalizations and stereotypes about others, providing a better basis for understanding and supporting the concerns they articulate, including by designing better policy. For example, if we compare the formerly neglected world of the suburban teenage drug dealers with the world of poor urban drug dealers described by Waverly Duck (2015), we not only come to understand both worlds in greater depth, but we also see that it might be more effective to target interactional processes and inequities linking drug-dealing and violent crime, rather than blaming individual drug dealers.

But sociologists usually want to do more than illuminate particular social worlds. Most cultural sociologists are also interested in exploring general *patterns* in subjective intention and reference, and how those patterns are influenced by interactional processes of meaning-making, both for the intending subject and for their interactional partners and audiences. They identify patterns of meaning-making in interaction which not only illuminate the particular social worlds they study, but also generalize to meaning-making in quite different social worlds. These patterns operate at different scales, from the individual to the crowd.

Regarding the individual, what Berger and Luckmann labelled primary socialization is now more often explored by cultural sociologists as cultivation of "*habitus.*" Pierre Bourdieu's (1977) *practice theory* has provided deep foundations for exploring the pre-conscious patterning of our attachments and attitudes – including tastes, identities, and skills – by taken-for-granted practices. In any given situation, people's intentions and references are shaped by their deeply ingrained habits.

Of course, people "know much more of their culture than they use," as Ann Swidler (2001, 13) famously observed, and different settings evoke different meaning-making, even for the same individual. Cultural sociologists interested in the meanings individuals bring to interaction also investigate *cultural repertoires* or *toolkits*, and variable strategies of action. Investigating cultural repertoires offers a way of exploring variation and flexibility in meaning-making in different contexts and at different times, even by the same individual.

Scaling beyond a focus on individual meaning-making processes forming intention and reference, cultural sociologists analyze interactional orders, or situations. Erving Goffman argued for a focus on interactional orders – "environments in which two or more individuals are physically in one another's presence" (1982, 2) – based in "cognitive presuppositions" about rules and norms. Broadening Goffman's idea beyond face-to-face interaction, Matthew Norton sees situations as "the temporal and spatial conjuncture of circumstances experienced by an actor at a given moment" (2014b, 162). In situations, the cultural propensities individuals bring to action meet the cultural forms available to offer the "definition of the situation" (Thomas and Thomas 1928, 571–2). Situations are the fundamental unit for understanding the intentionality and referentiality of culture in action. To help understand different sorts of situations, cultural sociologists analyze *idiocultures*, *subcultures*, *group styles*, *scenes*, and *performance*.

Many cultural sociologists who explore how interaction situations affect meaning-making examine meaning-making in face-to-face groups, exploring particular *idiocultures* and *subcultures*. Gary Alan Fine expands Goffman's concept of interaction order in time to encompass "recurring, meaningful, referential interaction" in conjunction with a shared past offered by small groups. A group sustains a specific "collective meaning system" or "idioculture" and similar groups form a subculture (Fine 2012, 160, 168). Brooke Harrington and Fine (2000, 313) argue that such small groups are "the organizing principle of social life" mediating social structure and individual action.

Beyond specific group subcultures, cultural sociologists investigate *group styles* and *scenes* as identifiable cultural patterns across different groups. Intended meaning and references in interaction are always implicitly shaped by three cultural features of group context which, according to Nina Eliasoph and Paul Lichterman (2003), pattern people's interaction. All groups have symbolic boundaries marking insiders from outsiders. They have shared understandings of their group bonds. And they have normative ways of speaking which influence their interaction. Identifying these three features of culture in group interaction allows us to compare cultural processes across different sorts of groups and identify group-level cultural similarities and differences. Similar features help us analyze similarities and differences in what Goffman would call "strips of action," or "scenes" within groups.

Scaling up from small group interaction, Goffman also foreshadows a more recent approach to analyzing larger-scale, more anonymous interaction processes as cultural *performance*. Jeffrey Alexander (2004) shows how to explain patterns in the ways that groups and individuals express for others the meanings of situations, and how those performances may succeed or fail.

Meaning-making involves intentionality and referentiality, which always emerge in particular contexts of action and interaction. Cultural sociologists have developed practice theories of *habitus* and of *cultural repertoires* to understand meaning-making in action. To scale up to meaning-making in group interaction, they examine *idiocultures*, *subcultures*, *group styles*, and *scenes*. On a larger scale, meaning-making in action, encompassing intentionality and referentiality, can be understood by analyzing *performance*.

Habitus and practice

Individuals are marked and shaped by their upbringing and experience. This fundamental sociological principle has a corollary: every individual brings ingrained capacities for particular forms of meaning-making to every situation they encounter, because of their socialization. Pierre Bourdieu labeled these capacities "habitus," and his theory of habitus is widely adopted to explain how society influences individuals' cultural capacities.

For Bourdieu, "habitus" is

> a system of lasting, transposable dispositions which, integrating past experiences, functions at every moment as a *matrix of perception, appreciation, and actions* and makes possible the achievement of infinitely diversified tasks, thanks to analogical transfers of schemes permitting the solution of similarly shaped problems. (1977, 82–3, original emphasis)

This means that our habitus is both powerful and flexible, and fundamentally generated by practices, considered apart from symbolic forms (Reckwitz 2002). It is powerful because it is subconsciously ingrained in us by our taken-for-granted practices, especially in early life. Bourdieu quotes Émile Durkheim to note that "in each of us, in varying proportions, there is a part of yesterday's man: it is yesterday's man who inevitably predominates in us, since ... he makes up the unconscious part of ourselves" (quoted in Bourdieu 1977, 79). Habitus is established less by conscious learning and more by subconscious practice. Each of us is inclined to express and prefer some types of meanings, symbolic forms, and interpretations over others, and this is natural and taken for granted, because of practices formed by our early life and social position.

Yet the habitus is also flexible: the schemas and ways of thinking inculcated by our practices are forms, not content, transferable to new contexts and new situations. That is, we are not only socialized with specific information and preferences but are also inculcated with ways of thinking which allow us to interpret new information and form new preferences. For example, many young people learn and obsess about every detail of their favorite sport or favorite team. Their habits of attention to this realm of detail can be transposed later to mastery of the detail of some quite different realm, like movie history or political policies. Similarly, perhaps early immersion in video games facilitates lateral learning of organizational and decision-making skills transferable to other realms. Treating politics or business like a competitive sport may not be the best way of promoting higher values or longer-term goals, but the frame is easily transposed from early experience and translates ways of thinking learned in childhood sports to adult realms.

Habitus links personal dispositions and capacities for meaning-making with broader social structures, especially social class. If, on average, people experience the same social conditions generating similar everyday practices, they will develop shared dispositions, and people in different class positions will develop a different habitus. So habitus is not simply the product of individuals' interaction – as in some earlier symbolic interactionist theories of socialization. This is because, for Bourdieu, "interaction itself owes its form to the objective structures ... which have produced the dispositions of the interacting agents and which allot them their relative positions in the interaction and elsewhere" (1977, 81). Social structures influence individual meaning-making capacities and dispositions through habitus.

In his famous study of habitus, *Distinction*, Bourdieu shows how differences in class habitus matter for cultural tastes. Tastes are often thought to be rather personal and idiosyncratic, but they are in fact deeply connected to individuals' and groups' class origins, and "the practical affirmation of an inevitable difference" (1984, 56). Class habitus influences aesthetic preferences, such as in visual arts and music, and also personal lifestyle, such as food, entertaining, clothing, cosmetics and beauty standards, and sports (Brisson and Bianchi 2017). For example, some sports are more accessible to those with elite backgrounds:

> [A]ll the features which appeal to the dominant taste are combined in sports such as golf, tennis, sailing, riding ... skiing ... or fencing. Practised in exclusive places ... , at the time one chooses, alone or with chosen partners ... , demanding a relatively low physical exertion that is in any case freely determined, but a relatively high investment ... of time and learning (so that they are relatively independent of variations in bodily capital and its decline through age), they give rise to highly ritualized competitions, governed, beyond the rules, by the unwritten laws of fair play. The sporting exchange takes on the air of a highly controlled social exchange, excluding all physical or verbal violence, all anomic use of the body ... and all forms of direct contact between the opponents. (Bourdieu 1984, 215, 217)

(And clearly, some of these features – the exclusion of physical violence, the absence of direct contact, the relative independence of physical, bodily capacities – contrast directly with requirements for the wrestling performances Barthes analyzed, often associated with poorer and less educated audiences.) Importantly, Bourdieu argues that these class tastes in sport – as well as foods, aesthetic tastes, and so on – are a matter not only of economic resources or barriers, but also of "more hidden entry requirements, such as family tradition and early training, or the obligatory manner (of dress and behaviour), and socializing techniques, which keep these sports closed to the working class" (1984, 217).

Bourdieu's analysis of the way habitus influences cultural taste has been developed and refined in many ways. For instance, Annette Lareau's (2012) influential study of class differences in child-rearing applied Bourdieu's insights to show how upper-middle-class parents' "concerted cultivation" of their children, scheduling organized activities and lessons and mediating institutional contexts, ultimately instills taken-for-granted skills for later success. And as we saw in chapter 1, Lauren Rivera (2015) examines how subtle, implicit bias based on cultural capital influences hiring for elite jobs, even for candidates with similar credentials.

Other developments in this line of research have extended some of Bourdieu's findings in new ways. For instance, although Bourdieu characterizes upper-class taste as exclusive, many sociologists have since found that broader "omnivore" tastes are generally more characteristic of higher classes: for instance, the capacity to enjoy a variety of different musical genres can be a form of exclusion (Bryson 1996; Hanquinet 2017; Lizardo 2017; Lizardo and Skiles 2015; Peterson and Kern 1996). In another influential extension, Michèle Lamont (1992, 2000) shows that class exclusion is based not only on cultural snobbery but also on moral judgements. And Jean-Pascal Daloz (2010, 2013) examines habitus, taste, and distinction in different countries, finding different ways of drawing elite boundaries – like presenting oneself as especially modest, or generous – in different political settings.

Regardless of the specifics, however, the connection Bourdieu demonstrated between class position and cultural taste continues to generate an influential program of socio-logical research on "cultural processes and causal pathways to inequality" (Lamont et al. 2014).

Cultural repertoires and strategies of action

While the idea of habitus helps account for how tastes, preferences, and identities are deeply shaped by an individ-ual's social background, the idea of *cultural repertoires* is important for understanding the wide variation in even a single individual's meaning-making, and their capacities for change. Ann Swidler challenges overly broad, all-encom-passing views of how culture influences action, pointing out that these generic views do not take account of selectivity, skepticism, and variation in the ways people relate to cultural elements:

> They do not simply express perspectives or values instilled in them by their culture. Instead, they draw from a multiform

repertoire of meanings to frame and reframe experience in an open-ended way. In debate, they may be selective, taking up any arguments that seem handy. In other situations, they take up one cultural frame ... until they run up against an unsolvable problem... . This frequent shifting among multiple cultural realities is not some anomalous sleight of hand but the normal way in which ordinary mortals ... operate. People know much more culture than they draw on in any one instance. ... And they slip frequently between one reality and another, switching the frames within which they understand experience. (2001, 40)

Because of this variation, Swidler argues that we should understand culture as a repertoire of elements from which individuals may select according to circumstances. (The term "toolkit" is sometimes used for the same idea, but the idea of selecting cultural elements from a toolkit connotes too much rational reflection, as opposed to pre-conscious expression, for most culture in action. As Stephen Vaisey [2009] argues, building on Swidler's model, cultural cognition is largely unconscious and schematic.)

So, for example, Swidler shows that love for a partner has two apparently contradictory meanings to people she interviews. Sometimes they talk about love as intense, effortless, and hyper-romantic, as in a movie or romance novel. This "mythic" connotation contrasts with an equally common idea that love is "prosaic," a matter of routine, everyday effort (Swidler 2001, 116–17). Many people use both meanings at different times, despite the apparent inconsistency.

Although Swidler's theory of cultural repertoires applies primarily to individual meaning-making in action, the concept may also be fruitfully applied to culture on a broader scale, and it helps avoid overly narrow and essentializing claims about group culture. Elsewhere (Spillman 1997) I show that national identities cannot be reduced to one or two core, unchanging symbols but are actually cultural repertoires encompassing a variety of symbolic elements which are used differently at different times. For instance, in the nineteenth century, Australians talked a lot about their political freedoms as distinctive, but that theme had faded a hundred years later. Similarly, in the nineteenth century, Americans talked a lot about their standing in the world; a century later, and even though they had become global leaders, few patriotic claims were made based on this status. Overall, both similar countries could draw on a repertoire of themes to characterize their national identity – such as standing in the world, political values and institutions, the land, founding moments, history, diversity, and ritual spectacle – but their claims about national identity varied according to situational purpose and historical context. National identity is a cultural repertoire, not a unitary meaning.

What patterns individuals' uses of their cultural repertoires? Swidler writes of individuals' "cultured capacities" – how practices embed individual predispositions to particular *strategies of action* – in a way that is coherent with, though broader than, Bourdieu's idea of habitus. Beyond individual predispositions, different interactional, institutional, and historical contexts will also affect how cultural repertoires are used in meaning-making (Abramson 2012; Swidler 2001).

For example, different sorts of interaction demand different degrees of symbolic elaboration, and so the interactional setting affects the extent to which people express the culture they actually know. And different interactional situations will also impose different demands for coherence: sometimes, consistent ideologies will be called for, but, more often, inconsistent amalgams of tradition or commonsense will suffice. Historically, more "settled times" – for an individual, or a society – will allow more reliance on taken-for-granted tradition or commonsense; more "unsettled times," by contrast, will demand meaning-making in the form of more explicit and coherent ideologies. And where institutions like marriage create practical dilemmas, people may draw on different and potentially contradictory elements of their cultural repertoire. For instance, Swidler argues that people think of "mythic love" in relation to the goal of finding a life partner, but "prosaic love" as necessary for decades of living with that person. Similarly, as we saw in chapter 1, Corey Abramson (2015) argues that dilemmas associated with aging generate a cultural repertoire of responses including different and sometimes contradictory ideas, such as bodily preservation or maximizing enjoyment, and general or specific social ties and obligations. Overall, consistent meaning-making driving action with overarching values is rare, and most likely to emerge in turbulent situations.

With the concepts of habitus and cultural repertoire, Bourdieu and Swidler offer contrasting but potentially compatible understandings of individual meaning-making in action: on one hand, meaning-making is influenced by people's ingrained habits and practices; on the other hand, their use of cultural elements is flexible and transposable according to context. Even though people bring particular cultural forms and ingrained experience as a background to each situation, and these predispositions are shaped by their social position, every situation also involves specific intentions and references which shape culture in action.

Idiocultures and subcultures

Beyond individual action, meaning-making is shaped by situated interaction. One of the most widespread and important types of situation shaping culture in action occurs in the group, in which individuals in repeated reciprocal interaction recognize each other as distinct individuals with shared experiences (Harrington and Fine 2000, 313). Group situations contrast with more anonymous or larger-scale social settings. Groups link individuals into the broader society: they are important for socialization of individuals, for originating social challenge and change, for diffusing innovations, and for establishing social status. In all this, "small groups are meaning-makers" (Harrington and Fine 2000, 320). Small, tight-knit groups like sports teams or congregations may possess "idiocultures" of shared symbols and norms which develop from their shared experience. Members recognize that they share experiences, symbols, and norms and can expect other members to understand them, even though outsiders may not.

Small groups come in infinite variety and offer rich opportunities for cultural sociologists interested in culture in interaction. They include groups focused on work, leisure, art, politics, and every other imaginable activity, and they include, more recently, not only face-to-face groups but also virtual groups online. Fine developed the concept of idioculture as he explored many small groups of different sorts, including, among others, little league players, mushroom collectors, weather forecasters, and chess players. To take one example, in his study of restaurant kitchens he shows how chefs and kitchen workers form tight-knit work groups and frequently characterize themselves as "family." Their closeness is expressed in nicknames, slang, memories, and jokes which distinguish them from outsiders. Teasing and pranks – like putting a hot sauce into a co-worker's drink – serve to emphasize shared experiences and express community: "[M]emories and reports of memory are shared by workers; this sharing connects them in a powerful web" (Fine 1996, 125).

As Fine notes, the idioculture of a single restaurant kitchen nests in a broader restaurant subculture (1996, 117). Workers who took a job in a new kitchen would lose the shared memories, nicknames, and jokes they might have enjoyed in their former workplace, but would recognize categories, symbols, norms, values, and rituals characteristic of the broader occupational subculture of restaurants. Members of a subculture may not interact with each other directly, but, like members of an idioculture, they share a distinct set of experiences which provide them with a shared set of communicative tools for meaning-making, distinguishing them from others. Some occupations may form subcultures, or what John Van Maanen and Stephen Barley (1984, 287) call "occupational communities": "people who consider themselves to be engaged in the same sort of work; whose identity is drawn from the work; who share with one another a set of values, norms and perspectives that apply to but extend beyond work related matters; and whose social relationships meld work and leisure." Fishermen, police officers, computer programmers, chefs – all participate in occupational subcultures based on their work lives. Elsewhere (Spillman 2012b, 149–80) I have shown how occupational community is expressed, too, by businesspeople who share an industry interest, such as concrete repair contractors, hospitality consultants, envelope manufacturers, and actuaries.

Subcultures exist everywhere, including in many unlikely corners of the social world, as these examples show. Among all these possibilities, sociologists have often been especially interested in youth subcultures and in musical subcultures, perhaps because they often display opposition to the mainstream (Bennett 2001, 2018; Hebdige 1979). Oppositional youth subcultures with a distinct argot and style and high symbolic boundaries have existed for many generations and continue to proliferate. As David Grazian points out, "American subcultures, including greasers, beats, folkies, hippies, surfers, punks, skinheads, b-boys, skate-boarders, riot grrrls, rave kids, and indie hipsters, have stood at the forefront of popular culture reinvention" (2017, 88).

Group styles and scenes

Interactive meaning-making in idiocultures and subcultures relies on categories, symbols, norms, values, and rituals generated in particular contexts and particular sets of inter-actions distinct from those shared by the larger society encompassing the groups. This is one way in which situa-tions affect meaning-making in practice. But many groups resemble each other, too, even if each seems unique to its members. Cultural sociologists analyzing situations and interaction also explore the ways in which types of group interaction are themselves patterned across idiocultures and subcultures. To understand broader patterns of group inter-action, Nina Eliasoph and Paul Lichterman analyze "group styles": that is, "recurrent patterns of interaction that arise from a group's shared assumptions about what constitutes good or adequate participation in the group setting" (2003, 737). These patterns may be shared across different groups.

Delving into these shared assumptions and treating them as durable cultural patterns, they discuss three important ways in which group styles might vary: in their boundaries, bonds, and speech norms. First, whom do members of the group see as outsiders, and how do they draw the boundaries of the group? Second, how do they understand what bonds them as insiders, and what do they assume about their mutual responsibilities? Third, what do they take for granted as appropriate (or inappropriate) ways of interacting in the group?

For example, studying different groups of religious volunteers, Lichterman (2005) found that groups varied in how well they could succeed in their good intentions of helping the disadvantaged, because they varied in how they understood their boundaries and bonds, and in how they talked about what they were doing. Some groups had high boundaries and did not actually understand much about the people they were trying to help, developing a sect-like isolation in spite of their intentions to reach out. Some group bonds demanded little of members and this "plug-in volunteering," with no clear understanding of other social worlds, could not make any longer-term difference for the disadvantaged (see also Eliasoph 2011, 117). Some groups allowed difficult, self-critical discussion and some did not: those with speech norms which allowed critical reflection were able to improve their capacities more than others.

What about interaction in groups which are not so clearly identified and bounded? How should we analyze interaction in situations within complex organizations, networks, and projects? Lichterman and Eliasoph suggest that even beyond clearly bounded groups, "scene styles" shape meaning-making possibilities. Like small groups, scene styles, too, may be analyzed in terms of their boundaries, bonds, and speech norms. The same scene style may be adopted in quite different settings. But even in the same organizational setting, participants may switch "scene styles" depending on context. For example, members of a network of youth groups switched between "club style," "service provision," "community of identity," and "social activism" definitions of their situation or scene style – interaction in the same group was not restricted to one style. At the same time, some scene styles, like the "community of identity" style, could be evident in very different groups (Eliasoph 2011; Lichterman and Eliasoph 2014, 829–33). To take an example from a very different sort of setting, Peter Levin (2004) found that financial traders in commodities futures sometimes adopted an interactional style focused on masculinized understandings of (apparently) gender-neutral competence, but in down times, when the market was slow, they switched to explicitly sexualized joking and banter. Gender hierarchy was understood differently in these different scene styles evident in the same group.

As they develop their concept of "scene style," and examine switching between scenes, Lichterman and Eliasoph build on Erving Goffman's analysis of interaction:

> As Goffman defines it, a "scene" is constituted by actors' implicit assumptions about "what is going on here" in this "strip of action." Thus we will focus on "scene style," how actors coordinate action in one scene; in any organization, there may be multiple "scenes" with multiple "styles." "Style" describes the making of a scene. (2014, 815)

An earlier use of Goffman's idea of "scenes" is important for analyzing specific musical subcultures. Musical subcultures come in different varieties, but some of the most well-known genres of music are "scene-based" – produced by a relatively small group of musicians for a local or virtual audience community (rather than a mass market) and expressing codified performance conventions and norms, style, argot, and "attitude," often challenging rival styles and mainstream manners (Lena 2012, 33). When musical subcultures are "scene-based," they also demonstrate what Lichterman and Eliasoph would analyze as distinctive boundaries, bonds, and speech norms. Musical scenes were once considered primarily local, identified with particular cities or neighborhoods, such as the Harlem jazz scene of the 1920s, the Seattle grunge rock scene of the 1990s, or the long-lasting country music scene in Nashville. But musical scenes may now also be translocal, like 1990s rave music scattered in cities around the world. And of course virtual musical scenes are proliferating (Grazian 2017, 89). Whether local, translocal, or virtual, musical scenes are "contexts in which clusters of producers, musicians, and fans collectively share their common musical tastes and collectively distinguish themselves from others" (Peterson and Bennett 2004, 1; see also Bennett 2001; Driver and Bennett 2014). David Grazian (2003) explores the complexities of just such a musical scene in his study of the Chicago blues scene, examining how local audiences, musicians, city boosters, and tourists contribute to and construct an ideology of blues "authenticity."

Performance

So far, all these approaches to understanding culture in interaction have focused on smaller-scale situations. But the situations we encounter are not always small-scale, face-to-face interactions (or their social media analogs). We also interact in anonymous settings and on a larger scale than groups and scenes. For example, large-scale interaction takes place in political campaigns, mass pilgrimages, mega-churches, protest demonstrations, and major sporting events like the Olympics or the World Cup. How can we analyze the patterns and contingencies of interactive meaning-making in a way which can encompass these larger-scale interactions?

Jeffrey Alexander offers a theory of performance which helps analyze the pragmatic contingencies of meaning-making in larger-scale as well as more personal interaction. Like many of the cultural sociologists mentioned earlier in this chapter, he also draws on Goffman's theory of interaction, but deepens the latter's analysis of performance by drawing from theater studies and expanding its application beyond the small-scale encounters Goffman (1959) analyzes. We can learn from theatrical analogies about individual and collective social performance – "the social process by which actors, individually or in concert, display for others the meaning of their social situation." By analyzing performance in depth, we can see whether and how they generate understanding and emotional connections for observers and audiences: "the conditions for projecting cultural meaning from performance to audience" (Alexander 2004, 529, 547).

Many factors may influence whether or not meaning is successfully communicated in performance. When performance works, audiences experience what Alexander terms "fusion," emotional connection, understanding, and a sense of authenticity. However, fusion is difficult to achieve, especially in complex societies including many different peoples, even though performance is ubiquitous.

Factors which can lead to successful or unsuccessful performance include the following:

- *Collective representations (background symbols and scripts).* For example, the performative success of the opening ceremony at the Olympics could be affected by whether or not it expressed shared cultural codes of global cooperation and competition, and whether or not scripted symbols like the Olympic torch and the images of national teams are clear and accessible. (What if national organizers relied entirely on their own national sporting symbols and history?)
- *Actors.* Performative success also relies on participants in the ceremony: torchbearers, speakers, teams, and other performers should seem natural and absorbed in the shared moment.
- *Audiences/Observers.* Do different *audiences* identify and engage with the performance, rather than remaining simply observers? Beyond those attending the ceremony, how does the performance play for those in the broader audience of the "media event" (Dayan and Katz 1994)? Does the local audience cheer at the right times? Do we see broadcasts of celebrity guests distracted from the proceedings? And how does critical media commentary interpret and assess the performance for broader audiences? For a global audience like an Olympics ceremony, simple symbols and engaged actors may be particularly important for crossing cultural boundaries.
- *Means of symbolic production.* Such means (in terms of appropriate places, times, props, costumes, etc.) should obviously be available. Cities and countries hosting the Olympics devote significant resources to producing a good show. For the Olympics more broadly, many cities conclude that resources for the extended performance of hosting an Olympics and showcasing their city are not available or better spent elsewhere.
- *Performance organization (mise-en-scène).* All the other elements of performance are mute without active organization to convey their message. So, for example, Olympic hosts often hire leading directors and producers to ensure a successful performance in their opening and closing ceremonies.
- *Social power.* Powers to produce, distribute, and evaluate performances also affect their success. Are scripts censored

by political authorities? Are producers starved of resources? Are there limitations on who may perform or attend? Who decides on distribution? (For instance, do TV network contracts allow easy widespread access?) And how do intermediate critics, like local broadcasters, affect audience engagement?

Like all culture in interaction, performance is contingent and variable, dependent on the intentionality and referentiality of meaning in context identified by Thompson (1990). So performance is a process with uncertain communicative outcomes. Performative power is critical in all areas of modern life and is becoming more central the larger the scale of mediated interaction becomes. Attempts to control performative success and failure are evident everywhere, from the micro-interactions analyzed by Goffman (1959, 17–77), such as in work worlds, like the interviewing for elite jobs Rivera describes (2015, 135–46); to widespread identities like gender (Butler 1999, 171–90; Goffman 1979); to critical social movements like those in Egypt and Hong Kong (Alexander 2011; Ku 2019); to the conversion of national cultural value into economic value (Bandelj and Wherry 2011, 11–12).

Of course, performance perspectives help cultural sociologists understand more about artistic settings, as well. For instance, Lisa McCormick shows how some collective representations of classical music performance – "prodigy," "virtuoso," "conquering hero," or "intellectual" – generate "cultural expectations of how the performer should look" in musical competitions, and may both constrain and enable successful performance. As she notes, women performers are constrained by the "conquering hero" script, for example, but the "prodigy" and "virtuoso" images were more easily incorporated in their performance (2015, 147, 154–5).

Understanding performance is especially crucial for analyzing modern political processes. For instance, political campaigners attempt to control as much uncertainty as possible – mobilizing resources, social power, and campaign experts – yet still face critical uncertainties in scripting, acting, and audience response. Even in the tightly controlled and highly resourced conditions of a presidential campaign, contingencies and errors of performance can make the difference between success and failure. As Alexander shows in his study of the 2008 US presidential campaign, one critical difference leading to Barack Obama's surprising victory was his performance of calm, thoughtful civil stewardship during a financial crisis, compared to his opponent John McCain's apparent impulsive and angry response (2010, 243–60; see also Mast 2019).

Indeed, many of the demands of leadership positions like the Presidency are performative, and became more so over the course of the twentieth century (Mast 2013, 18–42; Meyrowitz 1985). Analyzing the surprising failure of the impeachment of President Bill Clinton in 1998–9, Jason Mast demonstrates, for instance, that

> Clinton successfully performed himself into the role of a martyr who, threatened and wounded by undemocratic forces, labored through the Republicans' degradation ceremony in order to uphold the laws of the land for all of America... . As a social actor, Clinton was able to seize on contingent occurrences and turn them into symbolic events, to reweave, in his favor, the meaning-texture of American political and civic life. (2013, 152)

As Isaac Reed argues, successful performance generates its own power: "[S]ituated action and interaction exerts control over actors and their future actions" (2013, 203).

Conclusion

Cultural sociologists analyze meaning-making in action and interaction in order to understand its subjective and pragmatic dimension. People use symbolic forms with specific intentions and specific references in mind; because intentionality and referentiality are essential components of meaning-making, context and process matter for shaping meaning-making. Approaches to understanding how contexts pattern meaning-making range from those which examine individual action, through to those which examine small-scale and large-scale situations. Like approaches which analyze cultural forms, they deepen our understanding of unfamiliar others, help specify what groups share, clarify cultural difference, and help explain social conflict.

These approaches often build on sociology's long theoretical tradition of symbolic interactionism and methodological tradition of ethnography, and their newer inflections in practice theories. Erving Goffman's theoretical contributions have been particularly influential for recent approaches to understanding culture in interaction.

Some analysts of culture in action offer new ways of understanding what individuals bring to interaction – especially their *habitus* and cultural *repertoire*. People bring to every situation their ingrained habits and practices, shaped by their social position from an early age: their habitus shapes cognitive categories and evaluations available to them in new contexts. However, in any given situation, people can usually draw on a repertoire of possible interpretive frameworks, and which feels most comfortable to them depends not only on longstanding habitus but also on features of social context like institutional demands and whether it is settled or unsettled. For example, habitual predispositions ingrained since childhood may predispose someone to a taste for team or individual sports, but they might also include in the cultural repertoire they bring to new situations the interpretation of even individual sports as based on teamwork, should this make sense in light of surrounding institutional pressures.

Features of the *situation* are even more important for other sociologists who examine culture in interaction. Meaning-making is often a feature of groups, rather than simply individual processes, and groups link individuals into larger social settings. Small groups have shared *idiocultures* based on their members' shared history of interacting together. Shared experiences encapsulated in shared categories, symbols, norms, evaluations, and rituals which distinguish them from others are also characteristic of broader *subcultures* encompassing a number of similar small groups, often explicitly set against the broader society. So, for instance, a workplace may have a shared vocabulary and norms in face-to-face interaction which are hard for outsiders to understand; and even beyond face-to-face interaction, so, too, do occupational subcultures.

Cultural sociologists also consider general processes of group interaction, which may be shared in one way or another by quite disparate groups. *Group styles* are analyzed according to the bonds, boundaries, and speech norms they encompass. However, groups are not necessarily homogeneous in their interaction processes, and may also display varying *scene styles*, or strips of interaction, coordinated according to different bonds, boundaries, and speech norms – as in the differing approaches to gender hierarchy among traders in busy and quiet times.

While many approaches to analyzing culture in action and interaction highlight smaller-scale, often face-to-face, settings, larger-scale and more anonymous situations are also important, and increasingly so. With this in mind, some cultural sociologists analyze the contingencies and conditions of *performance*, which can apply to face-to-face interaction but easily scale up to shed light on culture in interaction on a larger scale, such as in electoral campaigns or media ritual events.

We saw in chapter 2 an array of conceptual tools which help cultural sociologists explore the ways convention and structure influence meaning-making. In this chapter, we have added a number of conceptual tools for analyzing the intentionality and referentiality of meaning-making in practice. Most in-depth cultural analysis will incorporate both angles on the topic, considering both cultural form and meaning-making in interaction. A third angle is also important: sociologists are always concerned with the ways the broader organizational context of meaning-making processes influences cultural forms and objects. In the next chapter we will explore how cultural sociologists approach this classic sociological question.

4
Producing Meaning

What do you need to know to do cultural sociology? We have seen so far that to investigate culture we analyze symbolic forms and interactional processes. Symbolic forms were not well analyzed in sociology until the emergence of the approaches we examined in chapter 2: this is the most important "value-added" of the subfield. By contrast, and as we saw in the previous chapter, cultural sociologists analyzing meaning-making in interaction build on and add to a deep sociological tradition of analyzing micro-social processes as they explore *habitus* and *practice, cultural repertoires* and *strategies of action, idiocultures* and *subcultures, group styles* and *scenes,* and *performance.* Cultural sociology also builds on another core sociological tradition: the idea that larger social structures explain our ideas and experiences. This tradition is the basis for the third important skill for investigating culture: analyzing how meanings are produced by the surrounding social organization and historical context.

As Berger and Luckmann pointed out when they analyzed "the social construction of reality," individuals are socialized to act "in the context of a specific social structure." For them, analyzing meaning-making at an individual or interactional level "must always have as its background a macro-social understanding of ... structural aspects." Institutions precede and shape our meaning-making; they "always have a history," they are experienced as objective realities, and they control our conduct. They are often reified to seem "independent of human activity and signification," and subject to extensive processes of legitimation. To fully understand meaning-making, we should investigate how it is influenced by its historical and institutional context (Berger and Luckmann 1966, 163, 163, 54, 90, 92).

So, for example, Roland Barthes (1972 [1957]) analyzed convention and structure in symbolic forms to explain how signs in wrestling matches expressed particular, melodramatic meanings: good, evil, suffering, justice, and defeat. Expanding on that illustration, we saw how cultural analysts focusing on situated interaction would pursue other questions: about the interactional processes involved in the socialization of the wrestlers; their interactions in backstage and frontstage contexts; and the variant interpretations of different audiences at different games. Based on what we saw in chapter 3, we could build beyond Barthes by analyzing the class habitus of wrestling audiences, for example, or the symbolic reper-toire of moral claims-making that wrestlers and audiences bring to their understanding of a match. We could analyze wrestling as a subculture, or think of the group style shared by wrestling and some other types of entertainment. Perhaps most appropriate to this particular subject, we could expand on Barthes' analysis by examining how features of perfor-mance are sometimes (but not always) synthesized to create a "fusion" between wrestlers and audience.

But such an account of wrestling in terms of symbolic form and interactional processes could still raise even more questions for cultural sociologists. Who organizes and promotes the matches, and how do their interests shape what happens? What is the market for wrestling as entertainment? How does wrestling fit into the broader industries of enter-tainment and sport, and do they influence how it changes? Are there legal or technological constraints affecting how a typical wrestling match proceeds? What influences wrestlers' career trajectories? Who are the main players in the field of wrestling, considered as a whole, and how is status allocated within that field? How did traditional wrestling turn into entertainment in modern capitalist societies? In short, how do broader features of social context influence meaning-making about wrestling?

All these questions suggest important dimensions of meaning-making beyond symbolic forms and interaction. As we will see, cultural sociologists thinking about the surrounding social context generating symbolic forms have developed many revealing accounts of how culture is influenced by changes in socio-historical context, how it is produced by organizations, and how it is generated in delimited fields of action. For instance, in one classic example, Richard Peterson (1990) analyzed how and why rock and roll became popular music in the 1950s, almost completely replacing an earlier jazz-based aesthetic of artists like Frank Sinatra, Nat King Cole, and Doris Day. He found that this was not a simple story of innovative musicians attracting a new generation of baby-boom listeners. In fact, Peterson argues that rock and roll could have remained very obscure if the organization of the music industry itself had not been changing. For example, new federal regulations opened up US radio licenses, and what had been a single national radio industry with four networks became more than a hundred autonomous local markets with eight or more stations each. Unable to afford expensive live programming, these stations began to rely on recordings, offering more space for previously obscure genres like rock and roll to receive airplay. According to this research, it is not enough to consider symbolic form and interactional context to explain the rise of rock and roll. If you are interested in contemporary culture, Peterson seems to suggest, you should follow the business news.

Many such studies of how culture is produced delve into the business of meaning-making. Answering questions about cultural production also involves examining how governments, professions, social movements, and transnational networks produce culture. This connects cultural sociology with fundamental sociological insights about how social structure shapes culture. This idea is shared to some degree not only by Berger and Luckmann but by all founding sociologists, and it is a taken-for-granted presupposition in many other areas of sociology.

However, cultural sociologists build on and expand this sociological principle by challenging the common assumption that big social structures themselves (like "capitalism" or "the nation-state") directly cause widespread ideologies ("reflection theory"). Rather, they examine the many and varied organizational forces which may generate different cultural outcomes within these broad social structures. They ask: how are shared cultural forms like categories, evaluations, narratives, and genres invented and circulated by organizations and networks with collective purposes beyond individual expression and interaction?

In this chapter, we focus on the conceptual tools cultural sociologists use to analyze processes of cultural production.

The socio-historical context of meaning-making: beyond reflection theory

Why do we sometimes expand the focus of our questions about meaning-making beyond symbolic forms and interaction? As we saw in chapter 2, analyzing symbolic forms in depth helps us understand more about the ways in which *conventions* and the *structure* of signification influence meaning-making. As we saw in chapter 3, analyzing interaction helps us learn more about how *intentionality* and *referentiality* in the use of symbolic forms influence meaning-making. But as John Thompson points out, a fifth feature of symbolic forms is also crucial. Symbolic forms are also "*contextual*" in ways that extend beyond interaction: they are "always embedded in specific socio-historical contexts and processes within which, and by means of which, they are produced, transmitted, and received." Symbolic forms "bear the traces ... of the social conditions of their production" (Thompson 1990, 145, 146).

If we all lived in small, undifferentiated, face-to-face groups with little outside contact almost all our lives, as was perhaps more common in pre-modern times, then the socio-historical contexts and processes shaping symbolic forms might be mostly restricted to the interaction processes we explored in the previous chapter. (Even so, we might wish to consider how specialized cultural producers – like religious officials, or other ritual specialists – might have a disproportionate impact on processes of meaning-making in the small group; and we might wish to delve deeper into forgotten ways in which the historical and ecological context had shaped our group's symbolic forms.) But obviously, most of us do not live in small, undifferentiated, isolated groups, and almost no-one has really done so for centuries. The structured social contexts in which symbolic forms are now embedded extend far beyond small groups, in both their scale and their temporal range.

Founding sociologists were all preoccupied in one way or another with the transition from traditional to modern societies, and they all offered ways to think about how the large social changes in emerging modernity created broad cultural changes. They also offered trenchant commentary about the cultural conflicts and cultural changes their societies faced. As their ideas were integrated into sociology, however, "culture" mostly came to be seen as a large-scale, macro-social property of entire societies: modern societies in general, capitalist societies in general, democratic societies in general, or entire nation-states. Sociologists mostly assumed that social structure determined culture, and therefore that culture reflected social structure. This assumption was pervasive not only in theories of ideology, which emphasized cultural power, but also in functionalist theories which highlighted how meaning-making supported social integration (Spillman 1995).

Some of the most innovative developments in cultural theory in the first part of the twentieth century were made by Marxist theorists who revised the theory of ideology to improve "reflection theory" to better understand cultural power. Many of these developments extended reflection theory to take better account of topics we have explored in previous chapters: symbolic forms (Lowenthal 1961; Lukács 1971 [1923]) and the dynamics of practice and interaction (Gramsci 1971; Williams 1973).

They also grappled with the impact of expanding mass communication and capitalist media industries on contemporary meaning-making. The emergence of mass communications was one of the most significant developments in the human history of meaning-making. As Thompson summarizes, this involved the appearance, in late fifteenth- and early sixteenth-century Europe, of a range of institutions concerned with the economic valorization of symbolic forms and with their extended circulation in time and space. ... [T]he production and circulation of symbolic forms was increasingly mediated by institutions and mechanisms of mass communication. This process of the mediatization of culture was pervasive and irreversible. ... And it is a process that continues to take place around us and to transform the world in which we live today. (1990, 162)

Beginning with the spread of new printing techniques in Europe from 1450, and the expansion of a commercial printing industry, and then continuing through the growth of a commercial press, and the twentieth-century development of broadcasting, processes of meaning-making changed fundamentally. The same transition happened elsewhere: for instance, Eiko Ikegami describes an "information revolution" in Tokugawa Japan when commercial publishing boomed after 1600 (2005, 286–323; see also Haveman 2015).

Thompson identifies four crucial and distinctive features of meaning-making in mass communication. First, the production and diffusion of symbolic goods is institutionalized in organizations and markets on a much larger scale than in the interactive meaning-making we saw in chapter 3. Second, there is a "fundamental break between the production and reception of symbolic goods." Unlike in a face-to-face meeting, the context in which you read this may be very different from the context of its composition. Third, in comparison with meaning-making in interaction, symbolic forms are accessible in many more different places and times. Fourth, in comparison with interactional meaning-making, mass communication involves the increasingly *public* circulation of symbolic forms (Thompson 1990, 220, 218–25). The fundamental outlines of this profound change remain in place today, even as the superficial customization and co-production of social media add another layer of constraint and possibility. Whereas in the distant past our experience of meaning-making was primarily interactional, much of it is now generated in more distanced, mediated forms.

Critical theorists Max Horkheimer and Theodor Adorno were among the first to reflect on the cultural impact of the radical changes in mass communications of the twentieth century, when media like movies, recorded music, radio, and TV emerged. For them, mass production of culture for capitalist markets by large corporations in concentrated industries meant an exponential increase in ideological domination in modern societies. They argued that when art and entertainment are commodified for the mass market in large, rationalized businesses, symbolic forms become formulaic, commercialized, imaginatively limited, and critically stunted: "[M]echanically differentiated products prove to be all alike in the end. That the difference between the Chrysler range and General Motors products is basically illusory strikes every child with a keen interest in varieties … . The same applies to Warner Brothers and Metro Goldwyn Mayer productions." For Horkheimer and Adorno, audiences became passive consumers dependent on mass-marketed cultural goods, conformist and uncritical. Regardless of whether consumers are critical, however, "the triumph of advertising in the culture industry" is that they "feel compelled to buy and use its products even though they see through them" (Horkheimer and Adorno 1972 [1944], 123, 167).

Many of these critiques still ring true today, especially considering the intensification of "surveillance capitalism" through social media (Zuboff 2018). Nevertheless, subsequent cultural sociologists have challenged overarching "reflection theories," such as in Horkheimer and Adorno's polemic. Reflection theories, they argue, overgeneralize, and seem to ignore the variable impact of specific processes of cultural production, circulation, and audience reception. For example, Paul DiMaggio (1977) developed an "organizational reinterpretation of mass culture theory" which identified different capitalist market conditions generating variations in cultural innovation and diversity. These conditions include not only concentrated monopolies homogenizing culture, as Horkheimer and Adorno and many others have noted, but also more variable production for segmented markets, and production of innovative and diverse symbolic forms in a competitive market environment with autonomous brokers between artists and organizational management. Cultural sociologists also challenged the assumptions that audiences were passive and "audience reception" was undifferentiated

(Bielby and Bielby 2004; Fiske 1992). So, even though many mass-produced symbolic forms might be explained as "reflections" of the capitalist organization of their production, the specific ways in which their production is organized cannot be ignored, and these differences are not captured in overarching theories of reflection. Even mass-produced music or movies vary in their innovation, and audiences may be creative in how they respond to them.

Overall, cultural sociologists have developed at least three important lines of analysis to better specify how socio-historical context influences culture, without making the overgeneralizations of "reflection theory." First, many turn to historical sociology to develop empirical studies and theoretical understandings of the problem of *cultural reproduction and change* in socio-historical context. This work suggests that the relation between context and culture should be analyzed as complex *articulation*, rather than reflection. Second, some analysts draw on the sociology of organizations in the *production-of-culture* perspective, as Peterson and DiMaggio do in the illustrations above. Finally, and perhaps most influentially, cultural sociologists often rely on *field theory*, developed most notably by Pierre Bourdieu. Each of these approaches offers a more specific way of understanding how socio-historical context influences meaning-making.

Cultural reproduction, change, and the problem of "articulation"

One rich line of investigation into how meaning is affected by its surrounding social environment unites cultural and historical sociology. (On historical sociology see Adams et al. 2005; Lachmann 2013.) Cultural sociologists are often more inclined than other sociologists to take history seriously. Recognizing that cultural phenomena are inherently historical, they often make history central to their theoretical and methodological assumptions and empirical inquiries. They ask about how cultural power is reproduced over time, and how cultural change is possible, including the large-scale historical changes which brought us modernity (and, perhaps, postmodernity [Gottdiener 1995; Jameson 1984]).

For example, in one of the most comprehensive efforts early in cultural sociology to develop answers to the question of how social environments influence meaning-making, and attempting to get beyond simple reflection theory, Robert Wuthnow identified three different ways that societies shape major cultural innovations: one set of conditions leads to new political, cultural, or religious understandings; a second set determines which of these innovations will be widely disseminated; and a third set influences which innovations will be successfully institutionalized, so that they last. Analyzing three major cultural innovations in European societies – the Reformation, the Enlightenment, and nineteenth-century socialism – he identifies an array of influences, including resource expansion, favorable institutions of cultural production and selection, and the active creation of discursive fields which are grounded in but transcend existing cultural forms. Most importantly, he shows in depth "the value of taking into careful consideration the actual circumstances in which ideological products were produced and disseminated rather than merely identifying general affinities between ideological patterns and broad features of the social environment" (Wuthnow 1989, 3, 541). The processes he studies are best labeled "articulation," not "reflection."

Around the same time, William Sewell (1992) asked a similar question about how change is possible given the power of social structure and ideology. Extending social theories developed by Anthony Giddens and Pierre Bourdieu, he argued that cultural schemas are built in to social structures, but that change is possible (in part) because these schemas are transposable to new and unexpected settings, and because apparently fixed social resources may have multiple meanings. Ideas do not simply reflect social structures, and active processes of meaning-making are sometimes indeterminate. So, he shows, the storming of the Bastille in the French Revolution generated new categories of French political culture in processes of re-signification (Sewell 1996).

Questions about the "articulation" between historical context and cultural change have attracted wide interest among cultural sociologists. This research deepens our understanding of political processes, economic action, popular culture, and the arts. Some cultural sociologists examine major, long-term political processes like state formation (e.g. Norton 2014a; Reed 2019; Steinmetz 1999; Xu and Gorski 2010), colonialism (Mukerji 2016, 73–90; Steinmetz 2007), nation formation (e.g. Bonikowski 2016; Elgenius 2011; Greenfeld 1992), and democratization (Alexander 2006; Fishman and Lizardo 2013). For example, Ikegami (2005) shows how the historical transition in Japan from feudal hierarchy to modern nation-state occurred with the rise of associational publics and was encouraged by shared artistic practices, like poetry readings, which muted status hierarchies. Elsewhere (Spillman 1997) I have explored how, much later, disparate and contentious groups of people came to share "nationalities" in the United States and Australia, and examined ways in which historical challenges in each country influenced particular meanings associated with those nations (see also Spillman and Faeges 2005). And Robert Fishman (2019) shows how differences in the way democratization took shape in Portugal and Spain in the late twentieth century generated different types of national economic policies decades later. These and many other similar studies grapple with understanding large-scale cultural reproduction and change by examining and theorizing particular processes of articulation between sociohistorical context and meaning-making, rather than taking for granted a simple process of reflection.

Cultural sociologists also analyze how historical context influences meaning-making in more particular political episodes and movements. For instance, contemporary life is shaped by the emergence of new understandings of social justice which emerged among reformers in Victorian Britain (Strand 2015) as well as by the much later influence of populist movements in Europe in the late twentieth century (Berezin 2009). Christina Simko (2015) shows the development of two different speech genres – "dualistic" and tragic – during episodes of national mourning in the United States, such as assassinations and terrorist attacks. Ellen Berrey (2015), meanwhile, explores how rhetoric encouraging racial diversity is actually shaped and paradoxically weakened in different organizational settings in the United States.

"Articulation" also helps us explain and understand economic culture better than "reflection," according to a growing body of research on industries and markets (Spillman 2012a, 159–66). In a study of the emergence of the modern industrial corporation as a dominant form of organization, William Roy showed that "institutions shape the taken-for-granted categories that reify frequently repeated social practices into 'things' like money, markets, corporations" (1997, 140). Such economic categories often vary cross-nationally, too. For instance, Frank Dobbin (1994) shows how differing socio-historical contexts lead to different ideas about "efficiency" by comparing emerging railway industries in England, France, and the United States. Similarly, by viewing "economic objects as cultural objects," Nina Bandelj (2008) shows how increasing foreign investment associated with globalization in the late twentieth century was interpreted differently, and could generate different sorts of active responses, in different East European countries.

Consumer markets are cultural constructions, emerging as new value is attributed to objects of exchange. Consumerism and critiques of consumerism emerged as a major cultural force in the twentieth century (Lury 2011; Warde 2015; Zelizer 2005). Cultural sociologists often examine how different socio-historical contexts generated and changed consumer markets. For example, Viviana Zelizer (1983) shows how consumers initially resisted life insurance, considering "preparing for death" or pricing a life distasteful; insurance companies responded to these beliefs by, for example, emphasizing family responsibility. (For a variant cultural framing, see Chan 2012.) Laura Miller (2006) traces conflicts between different understandings of book consumers in twentieth-century retail, while Daniel Cook (2004) traces the construction of children as consumers in the early twentieth century, and Tad Skotnicki (2017) analyzes how critics responded to the emergence of consumer markets around the same time.

Studies like these of how socio-historical context articulates with economic culture in varied ways support broader theories in economic sociology incorporating cultural perspectives. For example, Neil Fligstein develops a "political-cultural theory of markets," noting that markets are cultural projects involving property rights, governance structures, conceptions of control, and rules of exchange (2001, 70). More recently, Jens Beckert argues that capitalist dynamics rely on expectations about the future in many ways, and such expectations are shaped by discourses and communicative practices (2016, 13–14). These and other recent theories in economic sociology make productive use of the challenges to simplistic "reflection" theories of ideology which originated in cultural sociology.

Of course, popular culture, media, and the arts also attract extensive investigation by cultural sociologists interested in the articulation between socio-historical context and meaning-making. This was a central concern of critical theorists like Horkheimer and Adorno (deepening their analysis beyond their influential polemic noted above). As their colleague Leo Lowenthal argued in the mid-twentieth century, "popular culture is itself a historical phenomenon" and audiences' responses are "pre-formed and pre-structured by [their] ... historical and social fate" (1950, 332). For instance, he showed how themes of biographies in popular magazines shifted from work to leisure in the first half of the twentieth century, substituting "heroes of consumption" for the earlier stories about "heroes of production" as consumer societies emerged (Lowenthal 1961).

When contemporary cultural sociologists interested in popular culture examine how it is shaped by socio-historical context over time, they offer fresh perspectives of wide interest not only to sociologists, but also to fans (Darnesi 2019; Grazian 2017; Kidd 2014). Considering only musical genres, for example, fans of rap music will learn a lot from Jennifer Lena's (2012) research on the interactions between local producers and the music industry in the emergence of the genre. William Roy's (2010) study of American folk music shows different ways it was promoted by social movements in the twentieth century. By contrast to folk music, Richard Peterson (1997) examines how country music was shaped by the articulation between shifting industry organization, performance styles, and audiences. And Paul Lopes (2002) shows how musicians, fans, and others transformed jazz music from popular music to art in the mid-twentieth century. These studies are all deeply attentive to specific ways socio-historical context articulates with musical form and content, and how its impact changes.

As the social history of jazz indicates, the symbolic boundary between "popular culture" and "art" is shifting and contested. This observation has generated some core questions and foundational works for sociologists concerned with social context, articulation, and cultural change (Crane 1992a; Gans 1974). How does this important symbolic boundary get drawn, and how does it change? What gets to be categorized as art, and in what ways is that category ambiguous in practice? For example, Paul DiMaggio found that, in the United States, "the distinction between high and popular culture ... emerged in the period between 1850 and 1900 out of the efforts of elites to build organizational forms that, first, isolated high culture and, second, differentiated it from popular culture" (1982, 33; see also DiMaggio 1992). Along similar lines, Shyon Baumann (2001, 2007) examines why and how film came to be treated as art, as well as popular culture, in the mid-twentieth century. Ongoing, active cultural production both sustains and undermines common symbolic boundaries between genres labeled as art or popular culture.

Cultural sociologists also investigate how the arts themselves (however defined) articulate with socio-historical context and are especially concerned to avoid "reflection theory" by recognizing the autonomous realm of the aesthetic and examining historically its articulation with social organization (Alexander 2003; Alexander and Bowler 2014; de la Fuente 2007; Eyerman and McCormick 2006; Zolberg 1990). In doing so, they often explore well-known historical "art worlds" (Becker 1982). For instance, the changing social arrangements which supported the emergence of new artistic forms like impressionism in France in the late nineteenth century are analyzed by Harrison White and Cynthia White (1993 [1965]). Similarly, Diana Crane (1987) analyzes individual and organizational affiliations among four hundred artists to show how an expanding art world and changes in the social context of visual artists generated shifting "avant-garde" styles, such as abstract expressionism and pop art, in post-war New York. This central concern with the shifting boundaries of art worlds also helps analyze how "outsider art" – falling outside existing conventions and training networks – itself becomes canonized (Zolberg 2015; see also Fine 2004; Zolberg and Cherbo 1997), and changing understandings of how visual artists themselves understand the value of their aesthetic labor (Gerber 2017). Of course, the sociology of the arts also explores the articulation of socio-historical context with other aesthetic forms, including classical music (e.g. DeNora 1991; McCormick 2015) and literature (e.g. Childress 2017; Corse 1997; Griswold 1981, 2000, 2008).

So far, we have seen many ways in which cultural sociologists explore how the socio-historical context of meaning-making shapes symbolic forms. They offer systematic and extended studies of different types of political culture, economic culture, popular culture, and the arts. These contributions all move beyond theories about overarching "reflection" to specify particular, historically embedded moments and processes of "articulation."

This rich seam of historicized cultural sociology and the distinctive approach it offers to questions of articulation between social context and meaning-making have sometimes been neglected or taken for granted in overviews of the field. Certainly, other lines of research on culture discussed here may include historical elements to some degree, and they are not mutually exclusive. But research about the socio-historical context of meaning-making primarily grounded in approaches and methods shared with historical sociology is so widespread and consequential that it demands recognition as a distinct approach within cultural sociology.

The production of culture

Similar and related contributions and insights about social context and meaning-making are also offered in analytic perspectives more particular to cultural sociology, namely "production-of-culture" and "field" approaches. While they often draw on historical evidence, like the studies above, these perspectives focus on theoretically specified general features of socio-historical context important for understanding meaning-making.

Production-of-culture perspectives are best known for the way they analyze the impact of socio-historical context on popular culture and the arts, although they are sometimes also extended to other cultural products, such as science or religion (Crane 1992b). They encourage us to think about the varied impact of specific forms of organization for cultural production. For example, we have already seen above how industry changes influenced the origins of rock and roll, and how different culture industries can affect diversity and innovation in popular culture. Analytic approaches and insights from the sociology of organizations are applied to explain variation and change in cultural forms. This perspective was explicitly developed in response to the limitations of overarching reflection theories: it "challenged the then dominant idea that culture and social structure mirror each other" (Peterson and Anand 2004, 311).

Instead, production-of-culture theorists compared and differentiated cultural forms according to mid-range organizational processes influencing symbolic production, just as DiMaggio did in his organizational reinterpretation of mass culture theory mentioned above. So, for example, Paul Hirsch (1972) examined industry links and showed how brokers between artists and industry affected popular culture; Diana Crane (1976) showed how different reward systems in "invisible colleges" generated different kinds of scientific knowledge; and Howard Becker (1982) argued that we can see art as "collective action" developed through different types of cooperative links (or networks) and conventions (or genre-specific norms) and influenced by forms of support, distribution, evaluation, and regulation.

So although we typically experience symbolic forms and cultural products as consumers with particular demands and tastes, cultural sociologists draw attention to organizational factors influencing supply, rather than audiences influencing demand. Technological change is one well-recognized aspect of cultural production: for instance, new technologies often open new territories and create a demand for new content. The process we see in Peterson's study of rock and roll, above, by which the introduction of TV opened up more radio waves allowing more airplay, has often been repeated in the digital age, as with the rapid growth of streaming platforms creating space for the wider distribution of new or previously peripheral content (and this process also has deeper historical antecedents, as with the invention of the printing press [Eisenstein 1980]). Markets – especially as categorized and commensurated by producers, such as in industry rankings (Anand and Peterson 2000) – are another well-recognized influence in many forms of cultural production.

In addition to well-recognized influences like technologies and markets, some important "supply-side" factors affecting the nature of the symbolic products we access include the following:

Law and regulation. How are culture-producing organizations regulated? For instance, how is ownership and licensing of means of production (like animation software, or printing presses) set up? What about distribution, such as with radio licenses or cable channels? And how does that influence dominant cultural forms? Are there restrictions on media concentration? How does copyright and intellectual property law affect incentives for artists? Do laws and regulations censor particular types of content directly? Law and regulation set "ground rules that shape how creative fields develop" (Peterson and Anand 2004, 315). For example, Wendy Griswold (1981) challenges the assumption that nineteenth-century American novelists writing about the frontier were simply reflecting their society. In fact, the absence of copyright protections made English novels of manners cheaper for American publishers. When copyright protection was introduced in the late nineteenth century, the themes of American and English novels converged. Around a century later, copyright law changed cultural content again, discouraging the heavy sampling which had characterized hip-hop before the 1990s (Grazian 2017, 106). Many questions about cultural law and regulation constantly recur on the public agenda: should media companies merge? What rules should there be about censoring disturbing YouTube content? As answers to these questions shift, so too do familiar cultural forms.

Industry structure. Cultural products like popular music and TV shows may be more or less innovative or diverse according to whether industries are concentrated and vertically integrated, or composed of many smaller, competing producers, or something in between. Richard Peterson and David Berger (1975) argued that there were "cycles in symbol production," alternating between homogeneity in concentrated industries and episodes of competition and diversity. Paul Hirsch (1972) and Paul DiMaggio (1977) show that brokers and gatekeepers between artists, media companies, and markets can affect the diversity of cultural forms available in mass markets. Even as production and distribution of culture in small-scale online "scenes" proliferates beyond what was possible in twentieth-century culture industries, new questions emerge about how industry structure shapes widely available cultural content.

For example, the role of A&R (Artists and Repertoire) brokers connecting artists and record labels has changed as musicians can now connect with fans more directly; but A&R agents' role has diversified, and they may also develop, manage, and market talent (www.careersinmusic. com/what-is-a-r/; Lampel et al. 2000). Cultural sociologists like Peterson, Hirsch, and DiMaggio would predict, then, increasing innovation and diversity in popular music given this changed brokerage role.

Industries also share "conceptions of control," or norms about best strategies for success (Fligstein 2001). Conceptions of control in culture industries are generally aimed at managing market uncertainty. Overproduction – in the hope that an unpredictable few "blockbusters" will sustain the industry – is one commonly accepted strategy for minimizing uncertainty in culture industries. Other common strategies include reliance on "recombinant logic" (Gitlin 2000), formulaic genres, spinoffs, and artists with name recognition (Bielby and Bielby 1994).

Organizational structure. Generally speaking, cultural sociologists argue that more bureaucratic, hierarchical, functionally differentiated organizations can efficiently mass-produce and market standardized products – like textbooks, or movie-themed merchandise – over sustained periods. Small, diversified, nimble organizations – "job-shops" or solo producers – are better for smaller-scale, more innovative "craft" production. For instance, when comic books were published for the mass market from the 1930s to the 1980s, production was organized in assembly lines on an industrial scale, with dozens of writers and artists working on multiple titles. Later, when comic books were seen as counter-cultural art, production was organized around "independent publishers" and "well-paid auteur comic artists" (Lopes 2009, 12–13, 102–3).

However, large firms can subvert the homogenizing effects of their organization with multiple independent subdivisions, and yet accrue scale advantages like cross-division promotion (Lampel et al. 2000; Lopes 1992). And many culture industries now include both major players which are larger and more functionally differentiated, and a population of smaller players oriented to craft production and innovation. For instance, contemporary book publishing includes different types of organization: a "'federal' model allowed different, mostly autonomous publishing imprints within conglomerates to build specialized identities" and independent publishers with "fewer bureaucratic levels" which "sometimes contract out tasks like copyediting and cover design, and contract out their distribution" (Childress 2017, 118, 119).

Occupational careers. These are shaped by reward systems in culture organizations and industries. On one hand, many more people aspire to work in arts and entertainment than can sustain careers there. On the other, many culture industries rely on flexible labor for the strategic management of uncertainty. Occupational careers in these industries' oversupplied, flexible labor markets often involve short-term contracts for contingent, project-based work and high job mobility; strong reliance on reputational signals, peer network ties, and patronage; multiple job portfolios hedging occupational risk; and urban spatial concentration (e.g. Lingo and Tepper 2013; Mears 2011; Menger 1999; Rossman et al. 2010). Overall, occupational careers in cultural production combine traits of professional and small business tracks. Indeed, as Pierre-Michel Menger notes, flexible labor markets in performing arts foreshadowed the broader spread of contingent, flexible work relations in other industries (1999, 548). Brokers between artists and other industry players are also important for occupational careers. For instance, television writers challenge talent agencies, formally responsible for pursuing their best interests, when the latter begin to "package" writers with their other clients to make packaging fees from studios (Koblin 2019; cf. Bielby and Bielby 1999).

Investigation of all these factors has also expanded to address major trends in cultural production, such as digital co-production and globalization.

First, sociologists interested in examining the production of culture have expanded beyond the primary emphasis on culture industries. For example, Jennifer Lena (2012) distinguishes four types of musical genres based on different types of organization. In addition to "industry-based" cultural production, she analyzes "traditionalist," "avant-garde," and "scene-based" forms of organization. Traditionalist forms are organized in such settings as clubs, associations, festivals, tours, and educational institutions, with the goal of passing on an idealized heritage. Avant-garde forms emerge in local or internet-based creative networks, with experiment and innovation as the goals. Scene-based forms also emerge in local and virtual settings, with community formed around codifying subcultural style. This analytic framework easily extends to other cultural forms besides music and broadens analysis of cultural production beyond industry-based production to non-profit settings (like associations, clubs, and academia) and to interactional subcultures.

At a stretch, we can see any meaning-making in interactional subcultures as a sort of "co-production" (Peterson and Anand 2004, 324), but culture-in-interaction approaches discussed in chapter 3 already offer more precise conceptual tools for analyzing most subcultural meaning-making, including among consumers and fans. However, the rapid proliferation of scene-based cultural production of music and many other symbolic forms online does suggest that investigating "co-production" in its varying relations with the culture industries is an important line of investigation for production-of-culture scholars. For example, scenes like "underground bedroom pop" – a musical subculture of lo-fi, home-recorded videos created by teenage girls – invite the interest of music industry brokers: "[I]t probably won't be too long before a record label tries to manufacture a new pop artist with a lo-fi aesthetic" predicts "an A&R who has been keeping a close watch" (Petridis 2019).

Second, another important topic is globalized or transnational cultural production and distribution. "Media imperialism," with the export of cultural products like movies and music undermining local production owing to economies of scale, has long been a concern of media scholars and policy-makers. Another longstanding concern reverses the potential direction of influence: the value of global markets inclines Hollywood producers to favor easily diffused but more superficial action blockbusters or soaps over less easily translatable genres requiring verbal character development or verbal humor. However, "cultural production and dissemination do not occur in an unfettered way" and demand specific investigation of the relations between law and policy, industry structure, and organizational structure (Bielby 2010, 592). So, for example, Giselinde Kuipers (2015) shows how national institutions and norms of translation influence the impact of transnational cultural distribution. Denise Bielby and C. Lee Harrington, meanwhile, explore how television programs are syndicated to international buyers, examining the inner workings of global syndication events and organizations to identify "factors that facilitate or hinder the sale of television programs and concepts for global syndication" (2008, 20). Moreover, global regions of cultural production and distribution – such as South Asia or Latin America – may be a better unit of analysis than overarching globalization (Bielby 2010; Crane et al. 2002).

So cultural sociologists concerned with the production of culture identify specific features of social context which can shape cultural outcomes, especially in contemporary mass cultural production. They examine mid-range influences often absent in both popular discussion and overarching theories of reflection, including law and regulation, industry structure, organizational structure, and occupational careers. Following these threads, cultural sociologists offer many precise accounts of variation and change in the arts and popular culture which cannot be explained either by overarching reflection theories or simply by audience demand.

Cultural fields

Whereas the production-of-culture perspective offers tools to understand how socio-cultural environment influences meaning-making by analyzing the organization of production, showing what it includes and excludes, field theory broadens the scope of how cultural sociologists understand the relevant socio-cultural environment which explains meaning-making. The two approaches are similar and sometimes related in the way they reject overarching reflection theory and develop mid-range alternatives, but they do so in somewhat different ways.

Field theory itself takes several different forms (Fligstein and McAdam 2012, 23–31, 209–15; Martin 2003; Sallaz and Zavisca 2007). One line of thinking, neo-institutionalism, emerged in the sociology of organizations (DiMaggio and Powell 1991; Spillman 2012b, 111–21), highlighting the way taken-for-granted cultural infrastructure – cognitive categories and status evaluations – constitutes organizational "fields" orienting related organizations to each other. This culturally inflected perspective on organizations has been further developed and incorporated in the more recent "institutional logics perspective" (Thornton et al. 2012).

Scholars with an interest in culture and organizations have also developed a theory of "strategic action fields," synthesizing organizational insights with ideas and examples drawn from social movement studies, economic sociology, and political sociology. They analyze emergent or stable relationships between incumbent and challenger groups in a field. Field dynamics may be based on both cooperation and conflict, and they are often influenced by external fields, including the state. Cultural foundations – "conceptions of control" – are counted among the underlying conditions and causes of field stability and change. The theory of strategic action fields is most often used to understand organizational changes associated with social movements like the civil rights movement, and changes in industries (Fligstein and McAdam 2012, 114–63).

But most widely applied in cultural sociology is the field theory developed by Pierre Bourdieu. As with other field theories, the most relevant socio-cultural environment influencing meaning-making is not macro-structural or micro-interactional, but mid-range: configurations of individuals and groups mutually oriented to each other in some sort of common enterprise, such as an art, a science, or a profession. As Bourdieu summarizes field theory's challenge to "reflection theory":

> [B]etween the internal reading of the text which consists in considering the text in itself and for itself, and an external reading which crudely relates the text to the society in general … there is a social universe that is always forgotten, that of the producers of the works. … To speak of the field is to name this microcosm, which is also a social universe, but a social universe freed from a certain number of the constraints that characterize the encompassing social universe, a universe that is somewhat apart, endowed with its own laws, its own *nomos*, its own law of functioning, without being completely independent of the external laws. (2005, 33)

Members of a field share a common understanding of what is at stake in their shared activities – what Bourdieu calls the "*illusio*"– or an organizing logic or overarching principle. They also share, to some degree, taken-for-granted practices and know-how (see the discussion of habitus in chapter 3). Against this shared background, consciously or unconsciously, members of a field struggle competitively for status, prestige, and legitimacy. They may also struggle to define or change the criteria for allocating status. Actors in a field bring different material and ideal resources, or economic and cultural capital, to their practices and struggles in that field. Hierarchical field positions vary in their status and their reliance on different combinations of resources. Much of the meaning-making within a field may be autonomous, making sense mostly to those "in the know," and reliant on criteria and cultural capital internal to the field. However, some of the meaning-making will be "heteronomous," or influenced by forces external to the field, such as capitalist markets or the state. For example, a novelist may acquire prestige in the field of writers and literary critics, but that reputation could be undermined with a popular, money-spinning blockbuster.

As an analytic tool and a set of theoretical propositions about how the surrounding socio-cultural environment influences processes of meaning-making, Bourdieu's theory and its subsequent developments offer questions, hypotheses, and insights about many arenas of cultural production. As Monika Krause (2018) explains, we can investigate cultural fields at different scales, from the local to the transnational. We can analyze shared symbolic orders specific to and constituting a field. We can examine and compare differences in field autonomy, asking how much and how fields are influenced by external forces at any time. And we can investigate variations in their internal relational structure, asking about the ways in which they are hierarchical or competitive.

Many of Bourdieu's earlier writings on cultural fields focused on artistic fields, such as literature in France in the late nineteenth century (1993, 1996). He highlighted how status in an artistic field depended on challenging economic criteria with symbolic capital (as when Flaubert made a point of caring only about pure aesthetic issues), and connected positions in the field with social class. Many subsequent sociologists of the arts have investigated different local and national artistic fields, such as "underground" rap music (Oware 2014) or German writers (Anheier et al. 1995). Investigation has also expanded to global artistic fields. For instance, Larissa Buchholz (2018) argues that the global field of contemporary visual arts is best analyzed as a Bourdieusian field in which hierarchies have several different dimensions and dynamics, some more related to symbolic status, and some more related to market centrality. So, for example, China climbed rapidly in its share of the global auction market in visual arts in the decades before 2012, but the United States and Europe continued to dominate symbolic status, as indicated by the concentration of exhibition space.

Field analysis can also cast new light beyond the arts, looking at any self-constituted "social universe ... that is somewhat apart" and "endowed with its own laws" (as Bourdieu put it, above). Towards the more local end of the scale, for instance, Vanina Leschziner investigates the fields of elite cuisine in New York and San Francisco to understand the process of professional culinary creation. She argues that, unlike many artistic fields, these are geographically bound spaces with face-to-face interaction. Also unlike many artistic fields, commercial and artistic success are "largely fused": autonomy in the field is understood not as independence from external demands, but in terms of the ways chefs rely on the internal principles of the field to respond to heteronomous demands of their markets. Chefs pursue career paths and culinary styles with clear knowledge of a shared symbolic order and "rules of the game." They share a field logic of "flavor and originality," the "basic coordinates that structure a culinary field, determining where chefs, dishes, and culinary styles will be placed in the organizational space." They also demonstrate a direct personal understanding of hierarchy and competition in the field. Chefs select which principles to prioritize to guide their actions from their field positions, and struggle for the meaning and prestige afforded to their actions from those positions (Leschziner 2015, 144, 8, 127, 145; cf. Ferguson 2004).

Scientific fields have also interested scholars who investigate how field dynamics shape meaning-making (Bourdieu 1975). Within a particular scientific subfield, scientists will share some understanding of how to make legitimate claims for status, or, as Bourdieu puts it, "the monopoly of scientific authority." Many will compete for recognition within these terms. But some may also struggle over the current boundaries and definitions of the field. As Aaron Panofsky shows in his study of a chronically disorganized field, behavioral genetics, field analysis helps us see how "fields are the result of a set of struggles over boundaries and definitions rather than the unfolding of a unified idea." In his study, even "who counts as a behavior geneticist changes as boundaries, affiliations, and identities shift" (2014, 20). And where scientific knowledge is very highly contested in public, and thus heteronomous, scientific fields often involve disputes over knowledge claims among a wide variety of disparate actors. So, for example, Tom Waidzunas finds that knowledge claims about sexuality and "sexual reorientation" are made in a "field of therapeutics," which draws in numerous groups, such as "medicine, mental health (including psychiatry, psychology, and social work), and theology (especially the profession of religious counselling)" (2015, 25).

Scientific fields, highly contested or not, may operate at different scales, from the regional to the transnational. Most mainstream journalism, on the other hand, still takes place in fields at the scale of the nation-state (which was also Bourdieu's main focus). Rodney Benson compares journalistic fields in France and the United States to understand how socio-cultural context influences news stories about immigration. Journalistic fields comprise "the entire universe of journalists and news organizations relevant to a particular geographical region or political decision-making apparatus" (Benson 2013, 23). Somewhat like Leschziner, Benson finds that this field is not constituted with a clear opposition between autonomous and heteronomous forces, as Bourdieu proposed. Rather, journalistic fields are shaped by a tension between two heteronomous forces, civic and market. He argues that

> in both countries, nonmarket (civic) and market logics of worth and excellence vie for dominance. In France, however, the civic field, funded largely by the state, extends its reach over a larger portion of the field of power and encompasses more of the journalistic field... . Conversely, in the United States, the market field occupies a larger space within ... the journalistic field. (Benson 2013, 36, 48–60)

As a result, journalism is seen more as "debate ensemble"– a polemical debate of diverse viewpoints – in France and more as "dramatic narrative" in the United States. The difference has emerged historically because the two fields are differently positioned with respect to external demands from political, market, and civic powers. In their internal structure, however, journalistic fields in each country are more similar, with journalistic and audience habitus leaning to the more highly educated, in ways that influence the voices heard in the immigration coverage Benson studies (2013, 16, 60–6).

To take a final example of the range of topics encompassed by field theory, Joachim Savelsberg investigates differing responses to human rights violations, combining elements of Bourdieu's field theory with the theory of strategic action fields proposed by Neil Fligstein and Doug McAdam (2012), mentioned above. He compares three fields of professionals and organizations which define the problem differently. First, in the human rights field, including the International Criminal Court and many international non-government organizations like Amnesty, human rights violations are understood as crimes and "the logic of criminal law attributes mass violence to a small number of individuals." Second, humanitarian organizations, such as Doctors Without Borders, "highlight those aspects of suffering that can best be addressed by aid programs" and "emphasize long-term conditions ... and soft-pedal government actions that are immediate precursors, and likely conditions, of the violence." Third, diplomats focus even more on "long-term and structural causes of conflicts ... [and] avoid naming responsible actors" (Savelsberg 2015, 267, 269, 272).

These fields vary in the underlying logic of their under-standing of human rights violations because they differ in their autonomy from other political and social forces, which changes the specific context of meaning-making in each. Humanitarian organizations, and, even more, diplomats, are more reliant on governments where mass violence occurs than are human rights groups: "Humanitarian aid organizations depend on permits by lower-level government bureaucracies, where boundary-crossing professional solidarity may at times be at work. But in the diplomatic field dependency is yet more pronounced. Here actors depend on active partici-pation by high-ranking politicians of the country in which mass violence unfolds" (Savelsberg 2015, 272). Savelsberg also explores how these transnational fields' interaction with different nation-states can inflect the predominant meanings of human rights violations. In all instances, he empha-sizes how field participants "pursue specific goals such as justice, humanitarianism, and peace while they also seek to strengthen their own position within their respective field... . They thus buy into the field's ... matter of course assump-tions about the world" (Savelsberg 2015, 278).

So, influenced by field theory, many cultural sociologists analyze how specific features of social context can shape cultural outcomes in a wide variety of different settings – artistic, scientific, professional, political, and economic – at different scales, from the relatively local to the transnational. Members of a field are oriented to each other by a shared field logic somewhat distinct from other fields and not shared by outsiders to a field. Fields vary in their independence from external forces, in their relative balance of autonomy and heteronomy. Members of a field bring different economic and symbolic resources to their actions, and often struggle competitively for status within a field. Fields are dynamic not only in their shifting relations with external forces and internal status competition, but also in struggles over the definition of what is at stake in the field itself.

Conclusion

How does the surrounding socio-historical context influence meaning-making? Symbolic forms always emerge in a larger context of production, circulation, and reception. Exploring these processes, cultural sociologists build on a strong, widely shared sociological tradition which assumes that social structures determine culture. However, they also challenge this overly simplistic understanding of "reflection theory." Because reflection theory severely underestimates variability in the processes by which the surrounding social context influences meaning-making, and variability in the outcomes of those processes, cultural sociologists examine mid-range, mediating social arrangements influencing meaning-making. They do so in at least three distinct but compatible ways.

First, more than some other areas of sociology, cultural sociology takes history and historical inquiry seriously. A rich stream of research examines questions about *cultural reproduction and change* over time. It does so by examining what Robert Wuthnow called *articulation* between socio-historical context and symbolic forms. Cultural sociologists have contributed systematic, deeply researched accounts of large-scale historical changes like modernity; long-term political changes like state formation; changes in political culture such as populism; the emergence and change of industries and markets, including consumer markets; and the emergence of many different forms of popular culture and the arts, as well as the shifting symbolic boundary between the two.

Second, cultural sociologists have developed the *production-of-culture* perspective, drawing on insights from the sociology of organizations. This perspective challenges reflection theory by investigating how variable mid-range factors generate different symbolic forms, especially those produced in culture industries. It highlights the influence of *law and regulation*, *industry structure*, *organizational structure*, and *occupational careers* – as well as *technology* and *markets* – on what types of symbolic forms are produced, and especially the varying degree of innovation and diversity under different arrangements. Initiated with a focus on national mass culture industries, production-of-culture analysis may also extend to other sorts of cultural forms, including the arts; to social settings apart from industries, such as "scenes" (discussed in chapter 3); and to transnational systems of cultural production and circulation.

Third, for many cultural sociologists "the concept of a field is a research tool" for "the scientific construction of social objects" (Bourdieu 2005, 30). Although field theory comes in several different forms, the most influential in cultural sociology has been that of Pierre Bourdieu. *Field theory* challenges reflection theory by analyzing different field dynamics which mediate the relation between broad social structures and symbolic forms, and may be formed at different scales, from the local to the transnational. Fields are defined by a *shared logic*, recognized by all participants, and they vary in the degree and nature of their independence from external forces (or their *heteronomy/autonomy*). Members are mutually oriented to each other and to their shared field logic, but they may bring different symbolic and material resources (or *cultural and economic capital*) to their participation. Against this background, members struggle for status and position in the field, and may also struggle to redefine its focus and boundaries. Many cultural sociologists have applied field theory to understand how the surrounding socio-historical context influences many different genres of popular culture and the arts. Field theory has also been productive for understanding meaning-making in a variety of other settings, from the local to the transnational, such as the sciences, occupations and professions such as cuisine and journalism, and humanitarian aid.

This overview of different ways cultural sociologists explore how socio-historical context influences meaning-making adds to the overviews in previous chapters of how they analyze symbolic forms and meaning-making in interaction. As we saw in chapter 1, each of these elements – symbolic forms, interaction, and socio-historical context – is important for understanding meaning-making, and, taken together, they are both irreducible and compatible. The final chapter of this overview of what you need to know to do cultural sociology summarizes how to use them. Taken together, they offer a strong foundation for research on meaning-making

5
Conclusion: Landscapes, Stages, and Fields

What is cultural sociology? Throughout this book, we have seen that cultural sociologists analyze processes of meaning-making. After laying out this foundation in chapter 1, we subsequently explored three irreducible but compatible perspectives applied to this task: analyzing symbolic forms, meaning-making in interaction, and the broader socio-historical context of meaning-making. In this final chapter, we review and draw all these threads together, and go on to consider some of the ways we might weave them into new understanding and explanation of symbolic forms. As we have seen in many examples on topics ranging from music to war, such accounts can offer new knowledge about shared cultural assumptions, puzzling cultural differences, cultural domination, and cultural conflict.

Foundations and presuppositions of cultural sociology

The first requirement for understanding culture better is mindful recognition of the ways it surrounds us. Developing a critical sensitivity to rituals, symbols, evaluations, norms, and categories in social life is an essential habit for cultural sociologists. And such attention can be immediately rewarding, because much of what we take for granted in our everyday interaction – such as in our celebrations, clothing, musical tastes, speaking habits, and perceptions of people – assumes these sorts of expressive forms.

Second, it is useful to be aware of the history of the culture concept, and its different connotations, because its complexity sometimes makes it seem unduly confusing. Extreme variation in rituals, symbols, evaluations, norms, and categories, both across and within different social groups, is only the beginning of what can sometimes make culture puzzling. Historically, even the term "culture" has had several different connotations. Starting out in English as the name for a process, it came to refer to a general, abstract property of groups. Then, as a general, abstract category, the term could sometimes label a separate realm of expressive activities, apart from politics or economics, but at other times, it could refer to the whole way of life of a group. Cultural sociologists can investigate culture in either or both senses. But recognizing the genealogy of the term prevents unnecessary confusion.

Third, we can understand better how cultural sociologists situate their work within the discipline if we reflect on sociological traditions. Within the discipline, the concept of "culture" remained shadowy and ambiguous until the late twentieth century (unlike, for example, in anthropology). Ideas from early sociological theorists – like ideology, collective conscience, and interpretation – carried parts of its conceptual load in different ways. *The Social Construction of Reality*, Berger and Luckmann's classic of the sixties, came close to articulating a theory of culture building on sociological traditions, and "social constructionism" provided a widely accepted vocabulary for thinking about what might otherwise be called culture. But deep sociological disputes and ambiguities persisted. Sociologists debated whether to emphasize conflict or consensus; whether to focus on structure or agency; and whether to prefer interpretation or explanation. It helps to recognize these issues because they sometimes continue to generate doubts about the sociological value of analyzing "culture" for sociologists unfamiliar with more recent advances in cultural sociology. Familiarity with more recent cultural sociology can help address such doubts.

Recognizing these underlying sociological debates and themes also helps us understand the sorts of questions which interest cultural sociologists, more than other scholars of culture, such as questions about collective identities, class stigma, social movement narratives, culture industries, or political performance. All these topics and many others we have seen in previous chapters identify cultural phenomena of particular interest within sociological traditions.

Fourth, all these historical ambiguities suggest that any viable concept of culture should allow for complexity within coherence. The idea of culture as processes of meaning-making offers just such a coherent but capacious concept. By thinking of culture as meaning-making process, we avoid thinking of it as an abstract, general thing. We can also encompass both earlier connotations: the idea that it can be a separate realm of society, and the idea that it can be a property of whole groups. This concept can include a variety of different processes, such as ritualization, symbolization, evaluation, normative action, and categorization, as well as others that cultural sociologists may identify. It can help us investigate questions about consensus, domination, and conflict and questions about structure and agency in meaning-making in the real world, getting beyond scholastic disputation. And it can encourage both interpretation and explanation of symbolic forms. Considering culture as processes of meaning-making thus offers a coherent conceptual foundation for sociological investigation which yet leaves room for real-world and theoretical complexity.

Fifth, however, this breadth is not limitless. Cultural sociologists do assume that the human capacity for meaning-making is generic and that meaning-making is an essential part of all human groups and human action. But cultural processes are not reducible to biological processes. Nor are they reducible to subjective, individual, psychological experience. And nor can they be collapsed with or completely explained by large social structures, as "reflection theory" once assumed. While questions about how culture relates to each of these other realms are fundamental to social theory, cultural dynamics can and should be analyzed independently of biology, psychology, or social structure. Cultural sociologists presume that we must analyze culture as a distinct layer of reality or level of analysis.

Sixth, I have demonstrated in this book that cultural sociology includes three distinct but compatible lines of theory and research about meaning-making. The most distinctive approach, compared to other sociological subfields, is a focus on analyzing the properties of symbolic forms. Cultural sociologists may also analyze interaction as a meaning-making process, and in doing so they build on and add to interactionist traditions in sociology. The third approach considers how the surrounding socio-historical context influences meaning-making, developing longstanding sociological insights about how large social patterns shape our experience.

With cultural sociology firmly established, we now think about what Berger and Luckmann would have called "the social construction of reality" with many more differentiated and precise conceptual tools than we might have done in the sixties. These foundations and presuppositions which support them have proven highly productive of new knowledge about many topics of sociological interest.

Landscapes, stages, and fields

What do you need to know to do cultural sociology? The three important types of conceptual skills or approaches discussed in this book provide starting points for answering questions about culture. Depending upon the sorts of questions you might have, you may emphasize any one of these three approaches, and you may adopt different conceptual tools offered by each of them. You may also combine them in different ways. The three main lines of investigation – of symbolic forms, meaning-making in interaction, and meaning-making in socio-historical context – are productive in themselves, but are even more so when the different angles of vision are combined.

Table 1 summarizes the conceptual tools for doing cultural sociology surveyed here. The most important innovation cultural sociology offers is deeper and broader conceptual understanding of symbolic forms themselves, an important element of meaning-making which, as we noted in chapter 2, sociologists once tended to neglect. Drawing on many inter-disciplinary influences, including cognitive psychology, semiotics, literary criticism, and anthropology, cultural sociol-ogists offer new ways to analyze how conventions, symbolic structure, and materiality affect meaning-making. Conceptual tools developed to analyze this element of meaning-making include *cognitive categories, symbolic boundaries, schemas* or *frames, valuation* and *commensuration, discursive fields, binary codes, narrative, genre, materiality,* and *iconicity.* These various conceptual tools all offer ways of better analyzing features of symbolic forms which transcend any particular context, creating what Isaac Reed has called, metaphorically, "landscapes of meaning" (2011, 109).

Table 1. Conceptual tools for doing cultural sociology

Symbolic forms	Meaning in interaction	Producing meaning
Cognitive categories	Habitus	Reproduction/ Change
Symbolic boundaries	Repertoires	
Schemas/Frames	Strategies of action	Articulation
Valuation/ Commensuration	Idiocultures	Law and regulation
	Subcultures	Industry structure
Discursive fields	Group styles	Organization structure
Binary codes	Boundaries/Bonds/ Norms	Occupational careers
Narrative		Fields/Field logic
Genre	Scenes	
Materiality/Iconicity	Performance	Heteronomy/ Autonomy
		Forms of capital

Symbolic forms are also embedded in interactional contexts. They involve intentional action and contextual reference, as well as the convention, structure, and materiality which transcend specific situations. So the second essential element for understanding meaning-making is attention to meaning-making in interaction, explored in chapter 3. To investigate meaning-making in interaction, cultural sociologists build on deep micro-sociological traditions, including symbolic interactionist perspectives and ethnographic methods. Conceptual tools developed to analyze this element of meaning-making include *habitus* and *practice*, *symbolic repertoires* and *strategies of action*, *idiocultures* and *subcultures*, *group styles* and *scenes*, and *performance*. These various conceptual tools all offer ways of better understanding meaning-making in interaction. Since the work of Erving Goffman has been particularly influential for cultural sociologists interested in meaning-making in interaction, and Goffman is well known for his theatrical metaphors, we can think of this element of cultural sociology metaphorically as analyzing "stages" for meaning-making.

And symbolic forms are also embedded in broader socio-historical contexts. So the third essential element for understanding meaning-making involves attention to how meaning is produced by the surrounding social organization and historical context, beyond specific interactional situations, as explored in chapter 4. This line of investigation builds on fundamental sociological assumptions about how social structures shape culture, and the basic idea is widely shared across many sociological subfields. However, cultural sociologists specify overly general "reflection theory" in many ways. Conceptual tools developed to analyze this element of meaning-making include considering *cultural reproduction and change*, *articulation*, *the "production of culture"* (*including law and regulation, industry structure, organizational structure, and occupational careers*), *fields and field logic*, *heteronomy/autonomy*, and *cultural and economic capital*. These various conceptual tools all offer ways of analyzing how socio-historical context affects meaning-making. To continue our metaphorical place labels for the three elements of meaning-making, we can label this line of thinking as concerned with "fields" (while recognizing that it includes more than Bourdieusian perspectives.)

These lists distil and condense very extensive theoretical development and deep empirical study behind every concept, involving many career years of many cultural sociologists. Depending on the line of research you wish to follow, each concept functions as a portal into a rich set of theoretical resources and exemplary studies for any particular project. Many models for new projects can be found in the exemplars discussed in each chapter.

Exploring the cultural sociology of *What is Cultural Sociology?*

This book can serve as a convenient example to illustrate how research questions may be generated within the conceptual framework developed here, since it involves meaning-making processes shared by both author and readers. So suppose you were considering this book as an object of cultural analysis, or this book along with other similar overviews of socio-logical subfields.

First, you might consider various ways implicit conven-tions, cultural structures, and materiality make overviews like this meaningful. Depending on your research question, you might be interested in the ways conventional publishing industry *categories*, or *symbolic boundaries* between disci-plines and subfields, shape its content. You might consider the view of cultural sociology presented here as a *schema* or *frame* for understanding the subfield, a complex template for patterning interpretive elements in a way that is mentally accessible and memorable, strategically framed to promote cultural sociology. You might analyze the implicit processes of *valuation* and legitimation in the book, or consider formulas for *commensuration* with which this book might be rated and ranked alongside others.

Considering questions about persistent cultural structures, you might first consider how cultural sociology as a discourse is positioned within and shaped by sociology considered as a *discursive field*, examining what themes that positioning encourages, and what themes are discouraged or excluded. You could identify and trace *binary codes*, or fundamental categorical oppositions creating meaning, in that discursive field: meaning/structure, for instance, or collective/individual.

And although the book and others like it are primarily analytical in form, you might trace more implicitly here and more explicitly in related writings a progressive *narrative* of the emergence and expansion of cultural sociology as an area of sociology. You might consider the features of the short and comprehensive overview as a *genre* of text, compared to other genre forms.

Considering questions about materiality, you might consider how the *material form* the book takes can affect possibilities of action and interaction, stabilizing, preserving, or destabilizing meaning. How does your reading differ if the book takes traditional paper form compared to reading an e-book? How does meaning-making change if you are reading a heavily annotated second-hand copy, or interacting with other readers in electronic commentary? Which format preserves the ideas best, and when are they most destabilized? The question of *iconicity* is admittedly a stretch for any sociology book, but consider the allusions in this text to the iconic status of Berger and Luckmann's *Social Construction of Reality* among many sociologists. You may seek out a copy of that book, not to read, but for the compression of meaning through the aesthetic experience of the sixties classic as a material object.

But you may be less interested in how convention, structure, and materiality in symbolic forms affect meaning-making and more interested in meaning in interaction. We can broaden the focus, then, to think about what questions we might have about the processes of meaning-making as individuals and groups engage with this book (and others like it). First, even though this might be the first time you are encountering this book about cultural sociology, you and others will be bringing different dispositions to the encounter, structured by *habitus* developed in early subconscious practice. Maybe you have always been a reader, habitually absorbed by books, or maybe you are not particularly engaged by reading, but habitually more attentive to considerations like getting credit for an assignment. Quite possibly, you bring a *repertoire* of different ideas about "how to read" to meaning-making regarding this book, adopting different *strategies of action* according to whether the social context of your reading demands symbolic elaboration from you, maybe in a review, or you simply wish to note it in a routine way among many other books.

You might also ask how the *idioculture* of a class or other small groups may influence what the book means, and your experience of it. Perhaps your group's interaction order involves particular memories or nicknames which gives idiosyncratic meaning to some example or other in the text. Perhaps your membership in a *subculture* provides you with a shared set of interpretations or critiques not available to outsiders. Or perhaps your group operates with assumptions it shares with other groups, a *group style* defining *boundaries*, *bonds*, and *speech norms*, which could, for instance, either prohibit or encourage a critical approach. Maybe your group switches between "*scenes*," joking about outlandish questions at one time, developing new connections between examples at another. And although interaction surrounding a book rarely takes place in larger-scale *performance*, we might perhaps ask whether the background "scripts" it offers could support a teacher's successful "performance" in class, encouraging successful communication or audience fusion with the ideas.

Finally, regarding the third element of cultural sociology, you could explore how this book is shaped by its broader socio-historical context. That could include learning more about *cultural reproduction and change* in sociology as a discipline within the larger environments of the social sciences within higher education. What institutional and professional contexts encouraged the sustained production and institutionalization of cultural sociology? Was an initial phase of the production of diverse new ideas followed by a phase of selection in which some lines of inquiry were popularized and others relegated to the margins? What resources and institutional constraints shaped selection and institutionalization, influencing the *articulation* of cultural sociology with its surrounding social environment?

Or we could focus our questions about the impact of social context on this book and others like it by considering how it might be shaped by publishing *industry structure and organization*, along the lines of the *production-of-culture* perspective. Is it produced as part of an industry strategy of over-production? Does an autonomous publishing imprint with a specialized identity allow for authorial autonomy? What brokers mediate the relation between author and publisher? And how do industry and organizational constraints affect features like length and language? Further, to expand this line of investigation to consider sociology as a *field*, how *autonomous* is this book and the framework it offers within sociology's *field logic*; to what extent is it shaped by *heteronomous* economic demands from beyond sociology; and how does it position itself between the two? What *economic and cultural capital* are brought to its composition, production, and reception; what is the relative weight of each; and what is the book's impact on the *professional status and legitimacy* of author and publisher?

This is an extensive list of questions, and considering this book alone, many of them might seem rather trivial, and the answers not very puzzling. It would be essential to be selective about the combination of questions pursued, and develop pertinent comparisons, to give them their point. But they do demonstrate how the conceptual tools of cultural sociology can help open up new directions for developing research projects to understand and explain any process of meaning-making better, in many different ways. And as we have seen in many of the illustrations offered throughout this book (ranging from our first encounter with studies of bias in hiring in chapter 1 to our final encounter with the global field of humanitarian aid in chapter 4), new light can be shed on many more important sociological questions about consensus, domination, and conflict in social life by examining meaning-making in these different ways.

What is missing from *What is Cultural Sociology?*

Some of the illustrative leads above for investigating the "cultural sociology" of this book do suggest important reflections about what it does not do which may not be immediately obvious to many readers. To best use this book, it is important to be aware of its limitations and idiosyncrasies. Here, I want to highlight several implications of the symbolic boundaries and evaluations embedded in its writing, the national field of cultural sociology within which it has been produced, and the genre in which it has been composed. Cultural sociology's analytic tools can suggest how this book might be different in other possible worlds.

Implicit symbolic boundaries and evaluations are written into the text with the selection of core ideas, and, even more, in the selection of illustrations. While the overview is intended to be conceptually comprehensive, it is certainly true that the selection and emphasis of authors and examples could be very different, leading to different impressions of what counts as core knowledge in cultural sociology, and what the key references are. To take some rather straightforward examples of these inflections, this book underemphasizes the significance of heavily theoretical works in favor of conceptual contributions developed in systematic empirical studies. And it ignores important contributions and developments focused on the qualitative methodologies undergirding the systematic empirical studies. Both theory and methodology are significant and explicit concerns of cultural sociologists, subject to continuing innovation, and they sustain the strength of the subfield. In addition, some cultural sociologists also deepen those interests to explore philosophical debates about ontology and epistemology.

But for the purposes of providing a short overview which offers a foundation for practicing cultural sociology, these themes have been mostly excluded here. For this immediate purpose, written into the text is an implicit symbolic boundary between more abstract work focused on theory or methodology and work which also includes empirical inquiry, with the latter being evaluated more highly. In another possible world, there might be many more leads to theoretical and methodological discussion guiding each chapter. The hope, at least, is that there are enough leads to enable readers to delve deeper by pursuing theoretical discussions and debates influencing many of the authors here.

Second, this book is inevitably authored within a particular national field of cultural sociology, and best represents cultural sociology in the United States. Although disciplines like sociology are to some degree transnational, research is also shaped by different national fields and scholarly traditions, even when conducted in the same language. So, for example, what counts as core knowledge in cultural sociology, and what the key references are, will differ in different countries, even though there will also be many shared features. Some topics and ideas will receive greater emphasis; some may be minimized. Key authors may be neglected. Well-known examples could differ. So knowledgeable readers elsewhere – in the United Kingdom, France, Norway, China, or Australia, for example – will find themes emphasized differently and miss key references. A genuinely transnational overview of cultural sociology would be a very different book, involving more comparison and contrast than synthesis.

But the schema of cultural sociology offered here, and the genre of writing, could also help remedy its intrinsic national limitations. Unlike some scholarly overviews, this book does not introduce cultural sociology as a heroic narrative of important authors, their key works, and their battles. Although major ideas are certainly linked to leading scholars who develop them, the genre here is not heroic narrative but analytic synthesis, presenting an overall analytic framework that builds a coherent picture of the field. This framework is built around concepts, not people, and key works are illustrative rather than essential. This framework can be used flexibly across national contexts, even though this book draws mostly on cultural sociology in the United States. The framework can be used to think about and compare different thematic emphases, and how other authors use or combine the elements here. Each of the irreducible but compatible threads of cultural sociology – analyzing symbolic forms, meaning-making in interaction, and socio-historical context – could be developed and refined with other examples in other national contexts, and used to assess different thematic emphases, or position other significant authors or works. They could each be extended with ideas and exemplars generated in other professional fields, influenced by other processes of cultural production, or articulating differently with the surrounding socio-historical context.

Debates and difference among cultural sociologists

A third important omission is more deliberate, and some may consider it radical. Because this book aims at analytic synthesis, it ignores views of cultural sociology which pitch one approach against another in critical debate. Many potential points of dispute are possible. Familiarity with the main debates is important for assessing which of the many conceptual tools discussed here is appropriate to any particular empirical question. Fault lines of contention among scholars prioritizing each of the elements discussed here are summarized in Table 2.

Table 2. Debates among cultural sociologists

Challenger \ Target	Symbolic forms	Meaning in interaction	Producing meaning
Symbolic forms		Symbolic forms transcend situations	Symbolic forms impact meaning
Meaning in interaction	Underestimates varied interpretation		Underestimates situational meanings
Producing meaning	Underestimates social determinants	Underestimates macro-organization	

Some major fault lines divide those who prioritize analysis of symbolic forms (the most innovative line of inquiry from a sociological point of view) and those who prioritize analysis of the socio-historical context within which culture is produced (the most traditional line of inquiry from a sociological point of view). This dispute is sometimes characterized as pitting "cultural sociology" against "the sociology of culture." Those who prioritize the analysis of persistent symbolic forms argue that to focus entirely on the socio-historical context of meaning-making processes ignores the actual meanings involved. Those who prioritize the socio-historical context of meaning-making reply that in-depth analysis of symbolic forms can be too detached from the political and organizational dynamics shaping meaning-making.

Scholars who are most interested in analyzing symbolic forms may also suggest that focusing on interaction in context misses too much about the ways that symbolic forms transcend particular situations. Conversely, those who focus on meaning-making in interaction could argue that focusing strictly on symbolic forms underestimates the many, varied ways people might interpret symbolic forms in different situations.

Meanwhile, scholars most interested in the socio-historical context of meaning-making could argue that focusing on meaning-making in interaction underestimates the central significance of organized cultural production in modern, complex societies. By contrast, scholars who prioritize analyzing culture in interaction can argue that focusing on the socio-historical context of meaning-making processes makes too many assumptions about the actual meanings involved, which should be the focus of the analysis (similar to those who prioritize analyzing symbolic forms).

In brief illustration, we can suppose again that this book is the object of analysis by cultural sociologists. Some might focus on the symbolic forms it takes, such as its symbolic boundaries, schema, and genre. Others might challenge that focus by emphasizing its production within a circumscribed professional and industry setting. Those who emphasize symbolic forms would respond that some meanings transcend and shape context. Those who emphasize meaning in inter-action would argue that both other positions ignore important variation in what the book means according to interactional context. And so on.

And there could be other debates too, between scholars who work with different conceptual tools within each perspective. Preferences and allegiances, if not exactly debates, create further fault lines, for example, between those who emphasize the importance of cultural structures and those who analyze symbolic forms as simply conven-tional. Other preferences and allegiances might divide those who are more interested in the relative fixity of habitus and those who are more interested in the flexibility of repertoires. Other divisions could be excavated between those who are more interested in idiocultures and those who are more inter-ested in group styles. And while potential divisions between those who view socio-cultural context in historical terms, production-of-culture analysts, and devotees of field theory have not been canvassed, that may only be due to the fact the three approaches to understanding the impact of socio-historical context on meaning-making have been pursued in relative isolation until now.

These debates and disagreements can generate productive critique and help strengthen the conceptual resources contributed by different research programs to cultural sociology. Arguably, different approaches make different and potentially incompatible assumptions about what is real and important in social life, so the issues can go very deep. Familiarity with the comparisons and contrasts involved should be considered another important skill among those you need to know to do cultural sociology.

Nevertheless, this book ignores these debates and differences. Focusing on them would distract from its main purpose: providing an analytic overview which surveys and places in mutual relation many of the conceptual tools offered for the analysis of meaning-making in contemporary cultural sociology. The result can be considered more a menu than a competition. The question for readers is not which team to join, but which tools will help them explore meaning-making which interests them.

Using the conceptual tools of cultural sociology

Having become familiar with this conceptual menu, how should choices be made? Many of the studies mentioned as examples throughout this book offer leads and models. And any investigation could benefit by considering first and briefly the entire menu of questions raised by these conceptual tools, as in the illustration above of questions about this book. Such a survey can help assess which potential directions for investigation may be fruitful, and it can identify new lines of research.

Of course, projects will differ in their primary focus, too. Some important questions focus on symbolic forms. For specific topics, such as racial stigma or consumer preferences, looking at commonly shared conventional categories, symbolic boundaries, schemas/frames, or evaluations may be the best place to start. To understand symbolic forms at a more general level, though – such as those regarding humans in the natural environment, society and technology, or political culture – shared cultural structures (discursive fields, binary codes, narratives, and genres) should be examined across multiple social contexts. And a research focus on concrete cultural objects, such as bicycles or memorials, will invite analysis in terms of materiality and iconicity. Analysis of symbolic forms can be pertinent both to the more micro, cognitive level of social life and the more macro, historical level of social life.

If the primary focus is on meaning in interaction, questions about individual cultural propensities may be explored with concepts like habitus and repertoire. Questions related to group interaction, such as in a local foods cooperative or a congregation, may be explored with concepts like idioculture, group style, and scenes. And questions about larger-scale interaction orders, such as in self-help groups considered in general, or in political campaigns, should be explored by examining group styles or conditions of performance. Analysis of meaning in interaction is predominantly concerned with more micro levels of individual and group, but extends to more macro levels of social life with theories of group styles and of performance.

Whereas questions about meaning in interaction tend to lean towards the more micro level, questions about the socio-historical context of meaning-making tend to lean towards the larger scale. Questions about large-scale cultural change like democratization or marketization may be explored by examining specific historical processes of articulation. Questions about particular changes in cultural forms, such as in popular culture or professions, may be explored by examining the specific settings – of industry, organization, or field – in which they are produced.

So these are some places to start to pursue questions in cultural sociology by applying the core ideas discussed in this book. The choices you make will depend on whether you are more interested in landscapes, stages, or fields of meaning-making, and then also on your inclination to smaller-scale or larger-scale settings as you specify your research questions.

But even this menu may seem, quite rightly, a little restricted. While it is possible to focus primarily on one approach from within one of the three perspectives we have explored, a full understanding of any particular topic often involves more than one of these perspectives. Many insights and analytical payoffs can be achieved when scholars combine perspectives to examine links between symbolic forms and interaction, between symbolic forms and their socio-historical context, and between socio-historical context and processes of interaction. It is no accident that illustrations threaded throughout these chapters – such as those from studies of immigration news, elite chefs, sexuality debates, and musical genres – reappear in more than one context.

The analytical payoffs are multiplied when scholars weave together all three angles of vision. Some extended studies and major contributions touch on all three, even while highlighting one or the other. So, for example, a study of a music industry may also explore genre features and their connection to interactional scenes. Or a study of a profession will treat it as a field, but also examine the cognitive categories constituting its field logic, and the habitus of its members. Or a study of political codes and narratives will also explore the ways they are performed in major political events, and those events will be examined for the ways they articulate with the socio-historical context to encourage cultural reproduction or cultural change. In each of these illustrations, a more complete understanding of the topic emerges when analytic tools from each of the three types of cultural analysis we have discussed are combined. Although some scholars may consider the recommendation disrespectful of deeper scholarly commitments, the best strategy for fully exploring any research question is likely to be comprehensive: selecting analytic tools from each of the three sections of the cultural sociology "menu" to consider all three elements of meaning-making: symbolic forms, meaning in interaction, and socio-historical context.

But such comprehensive and multi-dimensional investigations of meaning-making are made possible by the precision and focus of all the conceptual tools we have reviewed. Sociologists who are interested in culture should no longer need to struggle to clarify what exactly they mean when they mention the term, or avoid it altogether. Nor should they be vague about the different elements that conducting a cultural analysis could entail. When Berger and Luckmann analyzed culture within the sociological tradition as "the social construction of reality" in the sixties, their book became a classic because it named an important phenomenon, connecting it to both micro-social processes like socialization and macro-social processes like legitimation already familiar in the discipline. Since then, sociology has developed many more precise ways of understanding the social construction of reality. Most importantly, interdisciplinary influences have helped create better ways of thinking more precisely about symbolic forms. Sociologists have also developed micro-social and macro-structural traditions in sociology in ways which address meaning-making. This book offers a stock-taking of how sociologists now understand meaning and meaning-making processes, demonstrating significant change and development.

Meaning-making is a fundamental human process and a generic human capacity. Since it is important in one way or another to everyone, it would be a sad omission if sociologists did not think about it too. From a sociological perspective, analyzing meaning-making can help us understand better what we share in our interactions and our groups, and how complex social organization is accomplished on a daily basis. It can help us understand cultural differences better. And by analyzing cultural processes, we can recognize and explain more about explicit social power, implicit social domination, difficult social conflict, and pressing social problems.

References

Abramson, Corey M. 2012. "From 'Either–Or' to 'When and How': A Context-Dependent Model of Culture in Action," *Journal for the Theory of Social Behaviour* 42(2): 155–80.

Abramson, Corey M. 2015. *The End Game: How Inequality Shapes Our Final Years*. Cambridge, MA: Harvard University Press.

Adams, Julia, Elisabeth Clemens, and Ann Shola Orloff (eds.). 2005. *Remaking Modernity: Politics and Processes in Historical Sociology*. Durham, NC: Duke University Press.

Adolphs, Ralph. 2009. "The Social Brain: Neural Basis of Social Knowledge," *Annual Review of Psychology* 60: 693–716.

Aiello, Giorgia. 2006. "Theoretical Advances in Critical Visual Analysis: Perception, Ideology, Mythologies, and Social Semiotics," *Journal of Visual Literacy* 26(2): 89–102.

Alexander, Jeffrey C. 2004. "Cultural Pragmatics: Social Performance between Ritual and Strategy," *Sociological Theory* 22(4): 527–73.

Alexander, Jeffrey C. 2006. *The Civil Sphere*. New York: Oxford University Press.

Alexander, Jeffrey C. 2010. *The Performance of Politics: Obama's Victory and the Democratic Struggle for Power*. New York: Oxford University Press.

Alexander, Jeffrey C. 2011. *Performative Revolution in Egypt: An Essay in Cultural Power*. New York: Bloomsbury Academic.

Alexander, Jeffrey C. and Philip Smith. 1993. "The Discourse of American Civil Society: A New Proposal for Cultural Studies," *Theory and Society* 22(2): 151–207.

Alexander, Jeffrey C. and Philip Smith (eds.). 2005. *The Cambridge Companion to Durkheim*. Cambridge: Cambridge University Press.

Alexander, Jeffrey C. and Carlo Tognato (eds.). 2018. *The Civil Sphere in Latin America*. Cambridge: Cambridge University Press.

Alexander, Jeffrey C., Ronald N. Jacobs, and Philip Smith (eds.). 2012. *Oxford Handbook of Cultural Sociology*. New York: Oxford University Press.

Alexander, Jeffrey C., Agnes Shuk-mei Ku, Sunwoong Park, and David A. Palmer (eds.). 2019a. *The Civil Sphere in East Asia*. Cambridge: Cambridge University Press.

Alexander, Jeffrey C., Anna Lund, and Andrea Voyer (eds.). 2019b. *The Nordic Civil Sphere*. Cambridge: Polity

Alexander, Victoria D. 2003. *Sociology of the Arts*. Oxford: Blackwell.

Alexander, Victoria D. and Ann Bowler. 2014. "Art at the Crossroads: The Arts in Sociology and the Sociology of Art," *Poetics* 43: 1–19.

Anand, N. and Richard A. Peterson. 2000. "When Market Information Constitutes Fields: Sensemaking of Markets in the Commercial Music Industry," *Organization Science* 11(3): 270–84.

Anderson, Elijah. 1999. *Code of the Street: Decency, Violence, and the Moral Life of the Inner City*. New York: W. W. Norton.

Anheier, Helmut, Jürgen Gerhards, and Frank P. Romo. 1995. "Forms of Capital and Social Structure in Cultural Fields: Examining Bourdieu's Social Topography," *American Journal of Sociology* 100(4): 859–903.

Bandelj, Nina. 2008. "Economic Objects as Cultural Objects: Discourse on Foreign Investment in Post-Socialist Europe," *Socio-Economic Review* 6(4): 671–702.

Bandelj, Nina and Frederick F. Wherry. 2011. "Introduction: An Inquiry into the Cultural Wealth of Nations," pp. 1–20 in Nina Bandelj and Frederick F. Wherry (eds.) *The Cultural Wealth of Nations*. Stanford, CA: Stanford University Press.

Barthes, Roland. 1972 [1957]. *Mythologies*, trans. Annette Lavers. New York: Hill & Wang.

Bartmanski, Dominik and Jeffrey C. Alexander. 2012. "Materiality and Meaning in Social Life: Toward an Iconic Turn in Cultural Sociology," pp. 1–12 in Jeffrey C. Alexander, Dominik Bartmanski, and Bernhard Giesen (eds.) *Iconic Power: Meaning and Materiality in Social Life*. New York: Palgrave Macmillan.

Baumann, Shyon. 2001, "Intellectualization and Art World Development: Film in the United States," *American Sociological Review* 66(3): 404–26.

Baumann, Shyon. 2007. *Hollywood Highbrow: From Entertainment to Art*. Princeton, NJ: Princeton University Press.

Becker, Howard S. 1982. *Art Worlds*. Berkeley and Los Angeles: University of California Press.

Beckert, Jens. 2016. *Imagined Futures: Fictional Expectations and Capitalist Dynamics*. Cambridge, MA, and London: Harvard University Press.

Benedict, Ruth. 1959 [1934]. *Patterns of Culture*. Boston: Houghton Mifflin.

Bennett, Andy. 2001. *Cultures of Popular Music*. Buckingham and Philadelphia: Open University Press.

Bennett, Andy. 2018. "Conceptualising the Relationship between Youth, Music and DIY Careers: A Critical Overview," *Cultural Sociology* 12(2): 140–55.

Benson, Rodney. 2013. *Shaping Immigration News: A French–American Comparison*. New York: Cambridge University Press.

Beresford, James and Ashley Bullard. 2018. "Narrating Policy: Potentials of Narrative Methods and Theories in Extending and Re-Orienting Policy Research." *Discover Society*. Social Research Publications. August 1. https://discoversociety.org/2018/08/01/focus-narrating-policy-potentials-of-narrative-methods-and-theories-in-extending-and-re-orientating-policy-research/

Berezin, Mabel. 2009. *Illiberal Politics in Neoliberal Times: Culture, Security, and Populism in the New Europe*. New York: Cambridge University Press.

Berger, Peter L. and Thomas Luckmann. 1966. *The Social Construction of Reality: A Treatise in the Sociology of Knowledge*. New York: Anchor Books.

Berman, Elizabeth and Daniel Hirschman. 2018. "The Sociology of Quantification: Where are We Now?" *Contemporary Sociology* 47(3): 257–66.

Berrey, Ellen. 2015. *The Enigma of Diversity: The Language of Race and the Limits of Racial Justice*. Chicago and London: University of Chicago Press.

Bielby, Denise D. 2010. "Globalization and Cultural Production," pp. 588–97 in John R. Hall, Laura Grindstaff and Ming-Cheng Lo (eds.) *Handbook of Cultural Sociology*. London and New York: Routledge.

Bielby, Denise D. and C. Lee Harrington. 2008. *Global TV: Exporting Television and Culture in the World Market*. New York: New York University Press.

Bielby, Denise D. and William T. Bielby. 2004. "Audience, Aesthetics and Popular Culture," pp. 295–315 in Roger Friedland and John Mohr (eds.) *Matters of Culture: Cultural Sociology in Practice*. New York: Cambridge University Press.

Bielby, William T. and Denise D. Bielby 1994. "All Hits Are Flukes: Institutionalized Decision Making and the Rhetoric of Network Prime-Time Program Development," *American Journal of Sociology* 99(4): 1287–313.

Bielby, William T. and Denise D. Bielby. 1999. "Organizational Mediation of Project-Based Labor Markets: Talent Agencies and the Careers of Screenwriters," *American Sociological Review* 64(1): 64–85.

Blair-Loy, Mary. 2003. *Competing Devotions: Career and Family among Women Executives*. Cambridge, MA: Harvard University Press.

Boltanski, Luc and Laurent Thévenot. 2006 [1991]. *On Justification: Economies of Worth*, trans. Catherine Porter. Princeton, NJ: Princeton University Press.

Bonikowski, Bart. 2016. "Nationalism in Settled Times," *Annual Review of Sociology* 42: 427–49.

Bourdieu, Pierre. 1975. "The Specificity of the Scientific Field and the Social Conditions of the Progress of Reason," *Social Science Information* 14(6): 19–47.

Bourdieu, Pierre. 1977. *Outline of a Theory of Practice*, trans. Richard Nice. Cambridge: Cambridge University Press.

Bourdieu, Pierre. 1984. *Distinction: A Social Critique of the Judgement of Taste*, trans. Richard Nice. Cambridge, MA: Harvard University Press.

Bourdieu, Pierre. 1991. *Language and Symbolic Power*, ed. and trans. John B. Thompson. Cambridge: Polity.

Bourdieu, Pierre. 1993. *The Field of Cultural Production: Essays on Art and Literature*. Cambridge: Polity.

Bourdieu, Pierre. 1996. *The Rules of Art: Genesis and Structure of the Literary Field*, trans. Susan Emanuel. Cambridge: Polity.

Bourdieu, Pierre. 2005. "The Political Field, the Social Science Field, and the Journalistic Field," pp. 29–47 in Rodney Benson and Erik Neveu (eds.) *Bourdieu and the Journalistic Field*. Cambridge: Polity.

Braunstein, Ruth. 2018. "Muslims as Outsiders, Enemies, and Others: The 2016 Presidential Election and the Politics of Religious Exclusion," pp. 185–206 in Jason L. Mast and Jeffrey C. Alexander (eds.) *Politics of Meaning/Meaning of Politics*. Cham, Switzerland: Palgrave Macmillan.

Brekhus, Wayne. 2003. *Peacocks, Chameleons, Centaurs: Gay Suburbia and the Grammar of Social Identity*. Chicago: University of Chicago Press.

Brekhus, Wayne. 2015. *Culture and Cognition: Patterns in the Social Construction of Reality*. Cambridge: Polity.

Brisson, Romain and Renzo Bianchi. 2017. "Distinction at the Class-Fraction Level? A Re-Examination of Bourdieu's Dataset," *Cultural Sociology* 11(4): 489–535.

Bryson, Bethany. 1996. "'Anything but Heavy Metal': Symbolic Exclusion and Musical Dislikes," *American Sociological Review* 61(5): 884–99.

Buchholz, Larissa. 2018. "Rethinking the Center–Periphery Model: Dimensions and Temporalities of Macro-Structure in a Global Field of Cultural Production," *Poetics* 71: 18–32.

Butler, Judith. 1999. *Gender Trouble: Feminism and the Subversion of Identity*. New York: Routledge.

Çaksu, Ali. 2017. "Ibn Khaldun and Philosophy: Causality in History," *Journal of Historical Sociology* 30(1): 27–42.

Cerulo, Karen. 1998. *Deciphering Violence: The Cognitive Structure of Right and Wrong*. New York: Routledge.

Cerulo, Karen (ed.). 2002. *Culture in Mind: Toward a Sociology of Culture and Cognition*. New York: Routledge.

Chan, Cheris. 2012. *Marketing Death: Culture and Life Insurance Markets*. New York: Oxford University Press.

Childress, Clayton. 2017. *Under the Cover: The Creation, Production, and Reception of a Novel*. Princeton, NJ, and Oxford: Princeton University Press.

Cook, Daniel. 2004. *The Commodification of Childhood: The Children's Clothing Industry and the Rise of the Child Consumer*. Durham, NC: Duke University Press.

Corse, Sarah. 1997. *Nationalism and Literature: The Politics of Culture in Canada and the United States*. New York: Cambridge University Press.

Crane, Diana. 1976. "Reward Systems in Art, Science, and Religion," *American Behavioral Scientist* 19(6): 719–32.

Crane, Diana. 1987. *The Transformation of the Avant-Garde: The New York Art World 1940–1985*. Chicago: University of Chicago Press.

Crane, Diana. 1992a. "High Culture versus Popular Culture Revisited: A Reconceptualization," pp. 58–74 in Michèle Lamont and Marcel Fournier (eds.) *Cultivating Differences: Symbolic Boundaries and the Making of Inequality*. Chicago and London: University of Chicago Press.

Crane, Diana. 1992b. *The Production of Culture: Media and the Urban Arts*. Newbury Park, CA: Sage.

Crane, Diana, Nobuko Kawashima, and Ken'ichi Kawasaki (eds.). 2002. *Global Culture: Media, Arts, Policy, and Globalization*. London: Routledge.

Daloz, Jean-Pascal. 2010. *The Sociology of Elite Distinction: From Theoretical to Comparative Perspectives*. New York: Palgrave Macmillan.

Daloz, Jean-Pascal. 2013. *Rethinking Social Distinction*. New York: Palgrave Macmillan.

D'Andrade, Roy. 1992. "Schemas and Motivation," pp. 23–44 in Roy D'Andrade and Claudia Strauss (eds.) *Human Motives and Cultural Models*. Cambridge: Cambridge University Press.

Darnesi, Marcel. 2019. *Popular Culture*. 4th ed. Lanham, MD: Rowman & Littlefield.

Dayan, Daniel and Elihu Katz. 1994. *Media Events: The Live Broadcasting of History*. Cambridge, MA: Harvard University Press.

de la Fuente, Eduardo. 2007. "The 'New Sociology of Art': Putting Art Back into Social Science Approaches to the Arts," *Cultural Sociology* 1(3): 409–25.

Debs, Mira. 2013. "The Suffering of Symbols: Giotto Frescoes and the Cultural Trauma of Objects," *Cultural Sociology* 7(4): 479–94.

DeGloma, Thomas. 2014. *Seeing the Light: The Social Logic of Personal Discovery.* Chicago: University of Chicago Press.

DeNora, Tia. 1991. "Musical Patronage and Social Change in Beethoven's Vienna," *American Journal of Sociology* 97(2): 310–46.

Dhaouadi, Mahmoud. 1990. "Ibn Khaldun: The Founding Father of Eastern Sociology," *International Sociology* 5(3): 319–33.

DiMaggio, Paul. 1977. "Market Structure, the Creative Process and Popular Culture: Toward an Organizational Reinterpretation of Mass-Culture Theory," *Journal of Popular Culture* 11(2): 436–52.

DiMaggio, Paul. 1982. "Cultural Entrepreneurship in Nineteenth-Century Boston: The Creation of an Organizational Base for High Culture in America," *Media, Culture and Society* 4(1): 33–50.

DiMaggio, Paul. 1987. "Classification in Art," *American Sociological Review* 52(4): 440–55.

DiMaggio, Paul. 1992. "The Extension of the High Culture Model to Theater, Opera, and the Dance, 1900–1940," pp. 21–57 in Michèle Lamont and Marcel Fournier (eds.) *Cultivating Differences: Symbolic Boundaries and the Making of Inequality.* Chicago and London: University of Chicago Press.

DiMaggio, Paul. 2002. "Culture and Cognition," in Karen Cerulo (ed.) *Culture in Mind: Toward a Sociology of Culture and Cognition.* New York: Routledge.

DiMaggio, Paul and Walter W. Powell. 1991. "Introduction," pp. 1–38 in Walter W. Powell and Paul DiMaggio (eds.) *The New Institutionalism in Organizational Analysis.* Chicago: University of Chicago Press.

Dobbin, Frank. 1994. *Forging Industrial Policy: The United States, Britain and France in the Railway Age.* New York: Cambridge University Press.

Douglas, Mary. 1966. *Purity and Danger: An Analysis of Concepts of Pollution and Taboo.* New York: Routledge.

Driver, Christopher and Andy Bennett. 2014. "Music Scenes, Space, and the Body," *Cultural Sociology* 9(1): 99–115.

Duck, Waverly. 2015. *No Way Out: Precarious Living in the Shadow of Poverty and Drug Dealing.* Chicago: University of Chicago Press.

Durkheim, Émile. 1995 [1912]. *The Elementary Forms of Religious Life*, trans. Karen Fields. New York: Free Press.

Eagleton, Terry. 1991. *Ideology: An Introduction.* London: Verso.

Eagleton, Terry. 2000. *The Idea of Culture.* Malden, MA: Blackwell.

Eisenstein, Elizabeth A. 1980. *The Printing Press as an Agent of Change: Communication and Cultural Transformation in Early Modern Europe.* Cambridge: Cambridge University Press.

Elgenius, Gabriella. 2011. *Symbols of Nations and Nationalism: Celebrating Nationhood.* New York: Palgrave Macmillan.

Eliasoph, Nina. 2011. *Making Volunteers: Civic Life after Welfare's End*. Princeton, NJ: Princeton University Press.

Eliasoph, Nina and Paul Lichterman. 2003. "Culture in Interaction," *American Journal of Sociology* 108(4): 735–94.

Epstein, Cynthia F. 1988. *Deceptive Distinctions: Sex, Gender, and the Social Order*. New Haven: Yale University Press; New York: Russell Sage Foundation.

Epstein, Cynthia F. 2007. "Great Divides: The Cultural, Cognitive, and Social Bases of the Global Subordination of Women," *American Sociological Review* 72(1): 1–22.

Espeland, Wendy. 1998. *The Struggle for Water: Politics, Rationality, and Identity in the American Southwest*. Chicago: University of Chicago Press.

Espeland, Wendy and Mitchell Stevens. 1998. "Commensuration as a Social Process," *Annual Review of Sociology* 24: 313–43.

Espeland, Wendy and Mitchell Stevens. 2008. "A Sociology of Quantification," *European Journal of Sociology* 49(3): 401–36.

Evans, J.A. 1982. *Herodotus*. Boston: Twayne.

Eyerman, Ron and Lisa McCormick (eds.). 2006. *Myth, Meaning and Performance: Towards a New Cultural Sociology of the Arts*. Boulder, CO, and London: Paradigm Publishers.

Farrell, Justin. 2015. *The Battle for Yellowstone: Morality and the Sacred Roots of Environmental Conflict*. Princeton, NJ: Princeton University Press.

Ferguson, Priscilla. 2004. *Accounting for Taste: The Triumph of French Cuisine*. Chicago: University of Chicago Press.

Fine, Gary Alan. 1996. *Kitchens: The Culture of Restaurant Work*. Berkeley: University of California Press.

Fine, Gary Alan. 2004. *Everyday Genius: Self-Taught Art and the Culture of Authenticity*. Chicago: University of Chicago Press.

Fine, Gary Alan. 2012. "Group Culture and the Interaction Order," *Annual Review of Sociology* 38: 159–79.

Fishman, Robert. 2019. *Democratic Practice: Origins of the Iberian Divide in Political Inclusion*. New York: Oxford University Press.

Fishman, Robert and Omar Lizardo. 2013. "How Macro-Historical Change Shapes Cultural Taste: Legacies of Democratization in Spain and Portugal," *American Sociological Review* 78(2): 213–39.

Fiske, John. 1992. "Audiencing: A Cultural Studies Approach to Watching Television," *Poetics* 21: 345–59.

Fligstein, Neil. 2001. *The Architecture of Markets: An Economic Sociology of Twenty-First-Century Capitalist Societies*. Princeton, NJ: Princeton University Press.

Fligstein, Neil and Doug McAdam. 2012. *A Theory of Fields*. Princeton, NJ: Princeton University Press.

Fourcade, Marion. 2011. "Cents and Sensibility: Economic Valuation and the Nature of 'Nature,'" *American Journal of Sociology* 116(6): 1721–77.

Fourcade, Marion. 2016. "Ordinalization," *Sociological Theory* 34(3): 175–208.

Frisby, David, and Mike Featherstone (eds.) 1997. *Simmel on Culture: Selected Writings*. London: Sage.

Furstenburg, Frank F., Jr., Sheela Kennedy, Vonnie C. McLoyd, Rubén G. Rumbaut, and Richard A. Setterstein, Jr. 2004. "Growing Up is Harder to Do," *Contexts* 3(3): 33–41.

Gans, Herbert. 1974. *Popular Culture and High Culture*. New York: Basic Books.

Gauchat, Gordon and Kenneth T. Andrews. 2018. "The Cultural-Cognitive Mapping of Scientific Professions," *American Sociological Review* 83(3): 567–95.

Geertz, Clifford. 1973. *The Interpretation of Cultures*. New York: Basic Books.

Gellner, Ernest. 1988. "Trust, Cohesion, and the Social Order," pp. 142–57 in Diego Gambetta (ed.) *Trust: Making and Breaking Cooperative Relations*. New York: Blackwell.

Gerber, Alison. 2017. *The Work of Art: Value in Creative Careers*. Stanford, CA: Stanford University Press.

Gieryn, Thomas. 1983. "Boundary Work and the Demarcation of Science from Non-Science: Strains and Interests in Professional Ideologies of Scientists," *American Sociological Review* 48(6): 781–95.

Gieryn, Thomas. 2002. "What Buildings Do," *Theory and Society* 31(1): 35–74.

Ginzburg, Carlo. 2017. "Civilization and Barbarism," *Sign System Studies* 45(3/4): 249–62.

Gitlin, Todd. 2000. *Inside Prime Time*. Berkeley: University of California Press.

Goffman, Erving. 1959. *The Presentation of Self in Everyday Life*. New York: Doubleday Anchor.

Goffman, Erving. 1979. *Gender Advertisements*. New York: Harper & Row.

Goffman, Erving. 1982. "The Interaction Order," *American Sociological Review* 48(1): 1–17.

Goffman, Erving. 2010 [1974]. *Frame Analysis: An Essay on the Organization of Experience*. Boston: Northeastern University Press.

Gottdiener, Mark. 1995. *Postmodern Semiotics: Material Culture and the Forms of Postmodern Life*. Oxford: Blackwell.

Gramsci, Antonio. 1971. "The Study of Philosophy," pp. 323–77 in Quinton Hoare and Geoffrey Nowell-Smith (eds. and trans.) *Selections from the Prison Notebooks*. New York: International Publishers.

Grazian, David. 2003. *Blue Chicago: The Search for Authenticity in Urban Blues Clubs*. Chicago: University of Chicago Press.

Grazian, David. 2017. *Mix It Up: Popular Culture, Mass Media, and Society.* 2nd ed. New York: W. W. Norton.

Greenfeld, Liah. 1992. *Nationalism: Five Roads to Modernity.* Cambridge, MA: Harvard University Press.

Griswold, Wendy. 1981. "American Character and the American Novel: An Expansion of Reflection Theory in the Sociology of Literature," *American Journal of Sociology* 86(4): 740–65.

Griswold, Wendy. 1987. "A Methodological Framework for the Study of Culture," *Sociological Methodology* 17: 1–35.

Griswold, Wendy. 2000. *Bearing Witness: Readers, Writers, and the Novel in Nigeria.* Chicago: University of Chicago Press; Princeton, NJ: Princeton University Press.

Griswold, Wendy. 2008. *Regionalism and the Reading Class.* Chicago: University of Chicago Press; Princeton, NJ: Princeton University Press.

Griswold, Wendy. 2013. *Culture and Societies in a Changing World.* 4th ed. Los Angeles: Sage.

Hall, John R. 2016. "Social Futures of Global Climate Change: A Structural Phenomenology," *American Journal of Cultural Sociology* 4(1): 1–45.

Hall, John R., Laura Grindstaff, and Ming-Cheng Lo (eds.). 2010. *Handbook of Cultural Sociology.* London and New York: Routledge.

Hanquinet, Laurie. 2017. "Exploring Dissonance and Omnivorousness: Another Look at the Rise of Eclecticism," *Cultural Sociology* 11(2): 165–87.

Harrington, Brooke and Gary Alan Fine. 2000. "Opening the 'Black Box': Small Groups and Twenty-First-Century Sociology," *Social Psychology Quarterly* 63(4): 312–23.

Haveman, Heather. 2015. *Magazines and the Making of America: Modernity, Community, and Print Culture, 1741–1860.* Princeton, NJ, and Oxford: Princeton University Press.

Hebdige, Dick. 1979. *Subculture: The Meaning of Style.* London and New York: Routledge.

Hirsch, Paul. 1972. "Processing Fads and Fashions: An Organization-Set Analysis of Culture Industry Systems," *American Journal of Sociology* 77(4): 639–59.

Hoang, Kimberly K. 2015. *Dealing in Desire: Asian Ascendancy, Western Decline, and the Hidden Currencies of Global Sex Work.* Oakland: University of California Press.

Horkheimer, Max and Theodor Adorno. 1972 [1944]. "The Culture Industry: Enlightenment as Mass Deception," pp. 120–67 in *Dialectic of Enlightenment*, trans. John Cumming. New York: Herder and Herder.

Hsu, Greta, Michael T. Hannan, and Özgecan Koçak. 2009. "Multiple Category Memberships in Markets: An Integrative Theory and Two Empirical Tests," *American Sociological Review* 74(1): 150–9.

Ikegami, Eiko. 2005. *Bonds of Civility: Aesthetic Networks and the Political Origins of Japanese Culture.* New York: Cambridge University Press.

Jacobs, Ronald N. 1996. "Civil Society and Crisis: Culture, Discourse, and the Rodney King Beating," *American Journal of Sociology* 101(5): 1238–72.

Jacobs, Ronald N. and Eleanor Townsley. 2011. *The Space of Opinion: Media Intellectuals and the Public Sphere.* New York: Oxford University Press.

Jacques, Scott and Richard Wright. 2015. *Code of the Suburb: Inside the World of Young Middle-Class Drug Dealers.* Chicago: University of Chicago Press.

Jameson, Fredric. 1984. "Postmodernism, or The Cultural Logic of Late Capitalism," *New Left Review* 146: 53–92.

Kane, Anne. 2000. "Reconstructing Culture in Historical Explanation: Narratives as Culture Structure and Practice," *History and Theory* 39(3): 311–30.

Kane, Anne. 2011. *Constructing Irish National Identity: Discourse and Ritual during the Land War, 1879–1882.* New York: Palgrave Macmillan.

Kidd, Dustin. 2014. *Pop Culture Freaks: Identity, Mass Media, and Society.* Boulder, CO: Westview Press.

Koblin, John. 2019. "Hollywood Awaits Fallout in Writers' Dispute," *New York Times,* April 15.

Krause, Monika. 2018. "How Fields Vary," *British Journal of Sociology* 69(1): 3–22.

Kreiss, Daniel. 2018. "The Fragmenting of the Civil Sphere: How Partisan Identity Shapes the Moral Evaluation of Candidates and Epistemology," pp. 233–41 in Jason L. Mast and Jeffrey C. Alexander (eds.) *Politics of Meaning/Meaning of Politics* Cham, Switzerland: Palgrave Macmillan.

Kroeber, A.L. and Clyde Kluckhohn. 1963 [1952]. *Culture: A Critical Review of Concepts and Definitions.* New York: Vintage Books.

Ku, Agnes Shuk-mei. 2019. "Performing Civil Disobedience in Hong Kong," pp. 84–103 in Jeffrey C. Alexander, Agnes Shuk-mei Ku, Sunwoong Park, and David A. Palmer (eds.) *The Civil Sphere in East Asia.* Cambridge: Cambridge University Press.

Kuipers, Giselinde. 2015. "How National Institutions Mediate the Global: Screen Translation, Institutional Interdependencies, and the Production of National Difference in Four European Countries," *American Sociological Review* 80(5): 985–1013.

Kuper, Adam. 1999. *Culture: The Anthropologists' Account.* Cambridge, MA: Harvard University Press.

Lachmann, Richard. 2013. *What is Historical Sociology?* Malden, MA: Polity.

Lamont, Michèle. 1992. *Money, Morals, and Manners: The Culture of the French and the American Upper-Middle Class.* Chicago: University of Chicago Press.

Lamont, Michèle (ed.). 1999. *The Cultural Territories of Race: Black and White Boundaries.* Chicago: University of Chicago Press; New York: Russell Sage Foundation.

Lamont, Michèle. 2000. *The Dignity of Working Men: Morality and the Boundaries of Race, Class, and Immigration.* Cambridge, MA: Harvard University Press; New York: Russell Sage Foundation.

Lamont, Michèle. 2012. "Toward a Comparative Sociology of Valuation and Evaluation," *Annual Review of Sociology* 38: 201–21.

Lamont, Michèle and Virag Molnar. 2002. "The Study of Boundaries in the Social Sciences," *Annual Review of Sociology* 28: 167–95.

Lamont, Michèle, Stefan Beljean, and Matthew Clair. 2014. "What is Missing? Cultural Processes and Causal Pathways to Inequality," *Socio-Economic Review* 3(1): 573–608.

Lamont, Michèle, Graziella Moraes Silva, Jessica S. Welburn, Joshua Guetzkow, Nissim Mizrachi, Hanna Herzog, and Elisa Reis. 2016. *Getting Respect: Responding to Stigma and Discrimination in the United States, Brazil, and Israel.* Princeton, NJ: Princeton University Press.

Lamont, Michèle, Laura Adler, Bo Yun Park, and Xin Xiang. 2017. "Bridging Cultural Sociology and Cognitive Psychology in Three Contemporary Research Programmes," *Nature Human Behaviour* 1: 866–72.

Lampel, Joseph, Teresa Lant, and Jamal Shamsie. 2000. "Balancing Act: Learning from Organizing Practices in Culture Industries," *Organization Science* 11(3): 263–9.

Lareau, Annette. 2012. *Unequal Childhoods: Class, Race, and Family Life.* Berkeley: University of California Press.

Lee, Hee-Jeong. 2018. "The Tension between Cultural Codes in South Korean Civil Society: The Case of the Electronic National Identification Card," *Cultural Sociology* 12(1): 96–115.

Lena, Jennifer. 2012. *Banding Together: How Communities Create Genres in Popular Music.* Princeton, NJ: Princeton University Press.

Leschziner, Vanina. 2015. *At the Chef's Table: Culinary Creativity in Elite Restaurants.* Stanford, CA: Stanford University Press.

Levin, Peter. 2004. "Gender, Work, and Time: Gender at Work and Play in Futures Trading," pp. 249–81 in Cynthia Fuchs Epstein and Arne L. Kalleberg (eds.) *Fighting for Time: Shifting Boundaries of Work and Social Life.* New York: Russell Sage Foundation.

Lichterman, Paul. 2005. *Elusive Togetherness: Church Groups Trying to Bridge America's Divisions.* Princeton, NJ: Princeton University Press.

Lichterman, Paul and Nina Eliasoph. 2014. "Civic Action," *American Journal of Sociology* 120(3): 798–863.

Lingo, Elizabeth and Stephen J. Tepper (eds.). 2013. "Patterns and Pathways: Artists and Creative Work in a Changing Economy," *Work and Occupations* 40(4).

Lizardo, Omar. 2012. "The Conceptual Bases of Metaphors of Dirt and Cleanliness in Moral and Non-Moral Reasoning," *Cognitive Linguistics* 23(2): 367–93.

Lizardo, Omar. 2017. "Improving Cultural Analysis: Considering Personal Culture in its Declarative and Non-Declarative Modes," *American Sociological Review* 82: 88–115.

Lizardo, Omar and Sara Skiles. 2015. "Musical Tastes and Patterns of Symbolic Exclusion in the United States 1993–2012: Dynamics of Conformity and Differentiation Across Generations," *Poetics* 53: 9–21.

Lopes, Paul. 1992. "Innovation and Diversity in the Popular Music Industry, 1969–1990," *American Sociological Review* 57(1): 56–71.

Lopes, Paul. 2002. *The Rise of the Jazz Art World*. Cambridge: Cambridge University Press.

Lopes, Paul. 2009. *Demanding Respect: The Evolution of the American Comic Book*. Philadelphia: Temple University Press.

Loveman, Mara, Jeronimo O. Muniz, and Stanley R. Bailey. 2012. "Brazil in Black and White? Race Categories, the Census, and the Study of Marginality," *Ethnic and Racial Studies* 35(8): 1466–83.

Lowenthal, Leo. 1950. "Historical Perspectives of Popular Culture," *American Journal of Sociology* 55(4): 323–32.

Lowenthal, Leo. 1961. "The Triumph of Mass Idols," pp. 109–40 in *Literature, Popular Culture, and Society*. Palo Alto, CA: Pacific Books.

Lukács, Georg. 1971 [1923]. *History and Class Consciousness*, trans. Rodney Livingstone. Cambridge, MA: MIT Press.

Lury, Celia. 2011. *Consumer Culture*. 2nd ed. Cambridge: Polity.

Martin, John Levi. 2003. "What is Field Theory?" *American Journal of Sociology* 109(1): 1–49.

Marx, Karl. 1978 [1846]. "The German Ideology," pp. 146–200 in Robert Tucker (ed.) *The Marx–Engels Reader*. 2nd ed. New York: Norton.

Mast, Jason L. 2013. *The Performative Presidency: Crisis and Resurrection during the Clinton Years*. Cambridge: Cambridge University Press.

Mast, Jason L. 2019. "Legitimacy Troubles and the Performance of Power in the 2016 US Presidential Election," pp. 243–66 in Jason L. Mast and Jeffrey C. Alexander (eds.) *Politics of Meaning/Meaning of Politics*. Cham, Switzerland: Palgrave Macmillan.

McCormick, Lisa. 2015. *Performing Civility: International Competitions in Classical Music*. Cambridge: Cambridge University Press.

McDonnell, Terence E. 2010. "Cultural Objects as Objects: Materiality, Urban Space, and the Interpretation of AIDS Campaigns in Accra, Ghana," *American Journal of Sociology* 115(6): 1800–52.

McDonnell, Terence E. 2016. *Best Laid Plans: Cultural Entropy and the Unraveling of AIDS Media Campaigns*. Chicago: University of Chicago Press.

Mears, Ashley. 2011. *Pricing Beauty: The Making of a Fashion Model.* Oakland: University of California Press.

Menger, Pierre-Michel. 1999. "Artistic Labor Markets and Careers," *Annual Review of Sociology* 25: 541–74.

Meyrowitz, Joshua. 1985. *No Sense of Place: The Impact of Electronic Media on Social Behavior.* New York: Oxford University Press.

Miller, Laura. 2006. *Reluctant Capitalists: Bookselling and the Culture of Consumption.* Chicago: University of Chicago Press.

Mora, G. Cristina. 2014. "Cross-Field Effects and Ethnic Classification," *American Sociological Review* 79(2): 183–210.

Mora, G. Cristina and Michael Rodríguez-Muñiz. 2017. "Latinos, Race, and the American Future: A Response to Richard Alba's 'The Likely Persistence of a White Majority,'" *New Labor Forum* 26(2): 40–6.

Mukerji, Chandra. 2009. *Impossible Engineering: Technology and Territoriality on the Canal du Midi.* Princeton, NJ: Princeton University Press.

Mukerji, Chandra. 2013. "Costume and Character in the Ottoman Empire: Dress as Social Agent in Nicolay's *Navigations*," pp. 151–69 in Paula Findlen (ed.) *Early Modern Things.* New York: Routledge.

Mukerji, Chandra. 2016. *Modernity Reimagined: An Analytic Guide.* New York: Routledge.

Mukerji, Chandra and Michael Schudson. 1991. *Rethinking Popular Culture.* Berkeley: University of California Press.

Mullaney, Jamie. 2001. "Like a Virgin: Temptation, Resistance, and the Construction of Identities Based on 'Not Doings,'" *Qualitative Sociology* 24(1): 3–24.

Nippert-Eng, Christena. 1996. *Home and Work: Negotiating Boundaries through Everyday Life.* Chicago: University of Chicago Press.

Nippert-Eng, Christena. 2010. *Islands of Privacy.* Chicago: University of Chicago Press.

Nisbet, Robert. 1993 [1966]. *The Sociological Tradition.* New Brunswick, NJ: Transaction Publishers.

Norton, Matthew. 2014a. "Classification and Coercion: The Destruction of Piracy in the English Maritime System," *American Journal of Sociology* 119(6): 1537–75.

Norton, Matthew. 2014b. "Mechanisms and Meaning Structures." *Sociological Theory* 32(2): 162–87.

Norton, Matthew. 2018a. "Meaning on the Move: Synthesizing Cognitive and System Concepts of Culture," *American Journal of Cultural Sociology* 7(1): 1–28.

Norton, Matthew. 2018b. "When Voters are Voting, What are They Doing? Symbolic Selection and the 2016 US Presidential Election," pp. 35–52 in Jason L. Mast and Jeffrey C. Alexander (eds.) *Politics of Meaning/Meaning of Politics.* Cham, Switzerland: Palgrave Macmillan.

Okin, Susan M. 1989. *Justice, Gender, and the Family.* New York: Basic Books.

Omi, Michael and Howard Winant. 1994. *Racial Formation in the United States from the 1960s to the 1990s.* New York: Routledge.

Ortner, Sherry. 1984. "Theory in Anthropology since the Sixties," *Comparative Studies in Society and History* 26(1): 126–66.

Oware, Matthew. 2014. "(Un)conscious (Popular) Underground: Restricted Cultural Production and Underground Rap Music," *Poetics:* 42: 60–81.

Panofsky, Aaron. 2014. *Misbehaving Science: Controversy and the Development of Behavior Genetics.* Chicago: University of Chicago Press.

Peterson, Richard A. 1990. "Why 1955? Explaining the Advent of Rock Music," *Popular Music* 9(1): 97–116.

Peterson, Richard A. 1997. *Creating Country Music: Fabricating Authenticity.* Chicago and London: University of Chicago Press.

Peterson, Richard A. and N. Anand. 2004. "The Production of Culture Perspective," *Annual Review of Sociology* 30: 311–34.

Peterson, Richard A. and Andy Bennett. 2004. "Introducing Music Scenes," pp. 1–15 in Andy Bennett and Richard A. Peterson (eds.) *Music Scenes: Local, Translocal, and Virtual.* Nashville TN: Vanderbilt University Press.

Peterson, Richard A. and David Berger. 1975. "Cycles in Symbol Production: The Case of Popular Music," *American Sociological Review* 40(2): 158–73.

Peterson, Richard A. and Roger Kern. 1996. "Changing Highbrow Taste: From Snob to Omnivore," *American Sociological Review* 61(5): 900–7.

Petridis, Alexis. 2019. "'Be Urself': Meet the Teens Creating a Generation Gap in Music," *The Guardian*, March 29.

Polletta, Francesca. 1998. "Contending Stories: Narratives in Social Movements," *Qualitative Sociology* 21(4): 419–46.

Polletta, Francesca, Pang Ching Bobby Chen, Beth Gharritty Gardner, and Alice Motes. 2011. "The Sociology of Storytelling," *Annual Review of Sociology* 37(1): 109–30.

Ragin, Charles C. and Lisa M. Amoroso. 2019. *Constructing Social Research: The Unity and Diversity of Method.* 3rd ed. Los Angeles: Sage.

Reckwitz, Andreas. 2002. "Toward a Theory of Social Practices: A Development in Culturalist Theorizing," *European Journal of Social Theory* 5(2): 243–63.

Reed, Isaac A. 2011. *Interpretation and Social Knowledge: On the Use of Theory in the Human Sciences.* Chicago: University of Chicago Press.

Reed, Isaac A. 2013. "Power: Relational, Discursive and Performative Dimensions," *Sociological Theory* 31(3): 193–218.

Reed, Isaac A. 2019. "Performative State-Formation in the Early American Republic," *American Sociological Review* 84(2): 1–34.

Rivera, Lauren A. 2015. *Pedigree: How Elite Students Get Elite Jobs.* Princeton, NJ: Princeton University Press.

Rohlinger, Deanna. 2015. *Abortion Politics, Mass Media, and Social Movements in America.* New York: Cambridge University Press.

Rossman, Gabriel, Nicole Esparza, and Phillip Bonacich. 2010. "I'd Like to Thank the Academy: Team Spillovers and Network Centrality," *American Sociological Review* 75(1): 31–51.

Roy, William. 1997. *Socializing Capital: The Rise of the Large Industrial Corporation in America.* Princeton, NJ: Princeton University Press.

Roy, William. 2010. *Reds, Whites, and Blues: Social Movements, Folk Music, and Race in the United States.* Princeton, NJ, and Oxford: Princeton University Press.

Sallaz, Jeffrey J. and Jane Zavisca. 2007. "Bourdieu in American Sociology 1980–2004," *Annual Review of Sociology* 33: 21–31.

Saussure, Ferdinand. 1990 [1916]. "Signs and Language," pp. 55–63 in Jeffrey C. Alexander and Steven Seidman (eds.) *Culture and Society: Contemporary Debates.* Cambridge: Cambridge University Press.

Savelsberg, Joachim. 2015. *Representing Mass Violence: Conflicting Responses to Human Rights Violations in Darfur.* Oakland: University of California Press.

Schroeder, Ralph. 1992. *Max Weber and the Sociology of Culture.* London: Sage.

Schudson, Michael. 1989. "How Culture Works: Perspectives from Media Studies on the Efficacy of Symbols," *Theory and Society* 18(2): 153–80.

Schwartz, Barry. 1981. *Vertical Classification: A Study in Structuralism and the Sociology of Knowledge.* Chicago: University of Chicago Press.

Sewell, William H., Jr. 1992. "A Theory of Structure: Duality, Agency and Transformation," *American Journal of Sociology* 98(1): 1–29.

Sewell, William H., Jr. 1996. "Historical Events as Transformations of Structure: Inventing Revolution at the Bastille," *Theory and Society* 25(6): 841–81.

Simko, Christina. 2015. *The Politics of Consolation: Memory and the Meaning of September 11.* New York: Oxford University Press.

Simmel, Georg. 1971. *On Individuality and Social Forms: Selected Writings,* ed. Donald Levine. Chicago: University of Chicago Press.

Skotnicki, Tad. 2017. "Commodity Fetishism and Consumer Sense: Turn-of-the-Twentieth-Century Consumer Activism in the United States and England," *Journal of Historical Sociology* 30(3): 619–49.

Smith, Christian. 2010. *What is a Person? Rethinking Humanity, Social Life, and the Moral Good from the Person Up.* Chicago and London: University of Chicago Press.

Smith, Philip. 2005. *Why War? The Cultural Logic of Iraq, the Gulf War, and Suez.* Chicago: University of Chicago Press.

Snow, David A., Robert D. Benford, Holly J. McCammon, Lyndi Hewitt, and Scott Fitzgerald. 2014. "The Emergence, Development, and Future of the Framing Perspective: 25+ Years since 'Frame Alignment,'" *Mobilization* 19(1): 23–45.

Spillman, Lyn. 1995. "Culture, Social Structure, and Discursive Fields," *Current Perspectives in Social Theory* 15: 129–54.

Spillman, Lyn. 1997. *Nation and Commemoration: Creating National Identities in the United States and Australia.* Cambridge: Cambridge University Press.

Spillman, Lyn. 2012a. "Culture and Economic Life," pp. 157–89 in Jeffrey C. Alexander, Ronald N. Jacobs, and Philip Smith (eds.) *Oxford Handbook of Cultural Sociology.* New York: Oxford University Press.

Spillman, Lyn. 2012b. *Solidarity in Strategy: Making Business Meaningful in American Trade Associations.* Chicago: University of Chicago Press.

Spillman, Lyn. 2016. "Culture," in George Ritzer (ed.) *The Blackwell Encyclopedia of Sociology.* 2nd ed. *Blackwell Reference Online*, November 29. DOI: 10.1111/B.9781405124331.2007.00003.x

Spillman, Lyn and Sorcha Brophy. 2018. "Professionalism as a Cultural Form: Knowledge, Craft, and Moral Agency," *Journal of Professions and Organization* 5(2): 155–66.

Spillman, Lyn and Russell Faeges. 2005. "Nations," pp. 409–37 in Julia Adams, Elisabeth S. Clemens, and Ann Shola Orloff (eds.) *Remaking Modernity: Politics and Processes in Historical Sociology.* Durham, NC: Duke University Press.

Steinmetz, George. 1999. *State/Culture: State-Formation after the Cultural Turn.* Ithaca, NY: Cornell University Press.

Steinmetz, George. 2007. *The Devil's Handwriting: Precoloniality and the Genesis of the Colonial State in Qingdao, Samoa and Southwest Africa.* Chicago and London: University of Chicago Press.

Stocking, George W., Jr. 1968. *Race, Culture and Evolution.* New York: Free Press.

Strand, Michael. 2015. "The Genesis and Structure of Moral Universalism: Social Justice in Victorian England, 1834–1901," *Theory and Society* 44(6): 537–73.

Swidler, Ann. 2001. *Talk of Love: How Culture Matters.* Chicago: University of Chicago Press.

Tavory, Iddo and Ann Swidler. 2009. "Condom Semiotics: Meaning and Condom Use in Rural Malawi," *American Sociological Review* 74(2): 171–89.

Thomas, William I. and Dorothy S. Thomas. 1928. *The Child in America.* New York: Alfred A. Knopf.

Thompson, John B. 1990. *Ideology and Modern Culture: Critical*

Social Theory in an Era of Mass Communications. Cambridge: Polity.

Thornton, Patricia H., William Ocasio, and Michael Lounsbury. 2012. *The Institutional Logics Perspective: A New Approach to Culture, Structure, and Process.* New York: Oxford University Press.

Vaisey, Stephen. 2009. "Motivation and Justification: A Dual-Process Model of Culture in Action," *American Journal of Sociology* 114(6): 1675–715.

Van Maanen, John and Stephen Barley. 1984. "Occupational Communities: Culture and Control in Organizations," pp. 287–365 in Barry M. Staw and Larry I. Cummings (eds.) *Research in Organizational Behavior*, Vol. 6. Greenwich, CT: JAI Press.

Vera, Hector. 2016. "Rethinking a Classic: *The Social Construction of Reality* at 50," *Cultural Sociology* 10(1): 3–20.

Wagner-Pacifici, Robin. 2010. "The Cultural Sociological Experience of Cultural Objects," pp. 110–18 in John R. Hall, Laura Grindstaff, and Ming-Cheng Lo (eds.) *Handbook of Cultural Sociology*. London and New York: Routledge.

Wagner-Pacifici, Robin and Barry Schwartz. 1991. "The Vietnam Veterans Memorial: Commemorating a Difficult Past," *American Journal of Sociology* 97(2): 376–420.

Waidzunas, Tom. 2015. *The Straight Line: How the Fringe Science of Ex-Gay Therapy Reoriented Sexuality.* Minneapolis: University of Minnesota Press.

Warde, Alan. 2015. "The Sociology of Consumption: Its Recent Development," *Annual Review of Sociology* 41: 117–34.

Weber, Max. 1998 [1904–5]. *The Protestant Ethic and the Spirit of Capitalism*, trans. Stephen Kalberg. 2nd ed. Los Angeles: Roxbury.

Weber, Klaus, Kathryn Heinze, and Michaela DeSoucey. 2008. "Forage for Thought: Mobilizing Codes in the Movement for Grass-Fed Meat and Dairy Products," *Administrative Science Quarterly* 53(3): 529–67.

White, Harrison and Cynthia White. 1993 [1965]. *Canvases and Careers: Institutional Change in the French Painting World.* 2nd ed. Chicago: University of Chicago Press.

Williams, Raymond. 1973. "Base and Superstructure in Marxist Cultural Theory," *New Left Review* 82(1): 3–16.

Williams, Raymond. 1976. *Keywords: A Vocabulary of Culture and Society.* New York: Oxford University Press.

Wood, Michael, Dustin Stoltz, Justin Van Ness, and Marshall Taylor. 2018. "Schemas and Frames," *Sociological Theory* 36(3): 244–61.

Wuthnow, Robert. 1989. *Communities of Discourse: Ideology and Social Structure in the Reformation, the Enlightenment, and European Socialism.* Cambridge, MA: Harvard University Press.

Wuthnow, Robert. 1992. "Infrastructure and Superstructure: Revisions in Marxist Sociology of Culture," pp. 145–70 in Richard Munch and Neil Smelser (eds.) *Theory of Culture*. Berkeley: University of California Press.

Xu, Xiaohong and Philip Gorski. 2010. "The Cultural of the Political: Towards a Cultural Sociology of State Formation," pp. 535–46 in John R. Hall, Laura Grindstaff, and Ming-Cheng Lo (eds.) *Handbook of Cultural Sociology*. London and New York: Routledge.

Zelizer, Viviana A. 1983. *Morals and Markets: The Development of Life Insurance in the United States*. New Brunswick, NJ: Transaction Publishers.

Zelizer, Viviana A. 2005. "Culture and Consumption," pp. 331–-54 in Neil J. Smelser and Richard Swedberg (eds.) *The Handbook of Economic Sociology*. 2nd ed. Princeton, NJ, Oxford: Princeton University Press; New York: Russell Sage Foundation

Zerubavel, Eviatar. 1981. *Hidden Rhythms: Schedules and Calendars in Social Life*. Chicago: University of Chicago Press.

Zerubavel, Eviatar. 1991. *The Fine Line: Making Distinctions in Everyday Life*. New York: Free Press.

Zerubavel, Eviatar. 1997. *Social Mindscapes: An Invitation to Cognitive Sociology*. Cambridge, MA: Harvard University Press.

Zerubavel, Eviatar and Eliot R. Smith. 2010. "Transcending Cognitive Individualism," *Social Psychological Quarterly* 73(4): 321–5.

Zolberg, Vera. 1990. *Constructing a Sociology of the Arts*. Cambridge: Cambridge University Press.

Zolberg, Vera. 2015. "Outsider Art: From the Margins to the Center?" *Sociologica & Antropologia* 5(2): 501–14.

Zolberg, Vera and Joni Maya Cherbo (eds.) 1997. *Outsider Art: Contesting Boundaries in Contemporary Culture*. Cambridge and New York: Cambridge University Press.

Zuboff, Shoshana. 2018. *The Age of Surveillance Capitalism*. New York: Public Affairs.

Zubrzycki, Geneviève. 2013. "Aesthetic Revolt and the Remaking of National Identity in Québec," *Theory and Society* 42(5): 423–75.

Zuckerman, Ezra. 2004. "Structural Incoherence and Stock Market Activity," *American Sociological Review* 69(3): 405–32.

Index